Arthur
Ransome
and
Captain
Flint's
Trunk

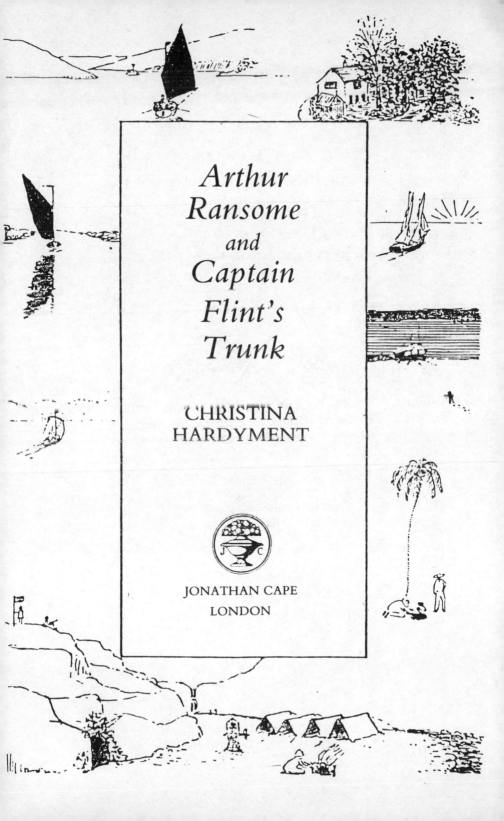

Arthur Ransome and Captain Flint's Trunk

CHRISTINA HARDYMENT

JONATHAN CAPE
LONDON

To my brothers,
Peter and John,
in memory of the years
spent in the Wilderness

SWALLOWS·AND·AMAZONS·FOR·EVER!

First published 1984
Reprinted 1988
First published in paperback 1988
Reprinted 1990
Copyright © 1984 by Christina Hardyment
Jonathan Cape Ltd, 20 Vauxhall Bridge Road, London SW1V 2SA

A CIP catalogue record for this book
is available from the British Library

ISBN 0 224 02989 4 (hardback)
0 224 02590 2 (paperback)

Phototypeset by Falcon Graphic Art Ltd
Wallington, Surrey
Printed and bound in Great Britain by
Hazell, Watson & Viney Ltd,
Aylesbury, Bucks

Contents

Illustrations

Plates

Illustrations

Maps

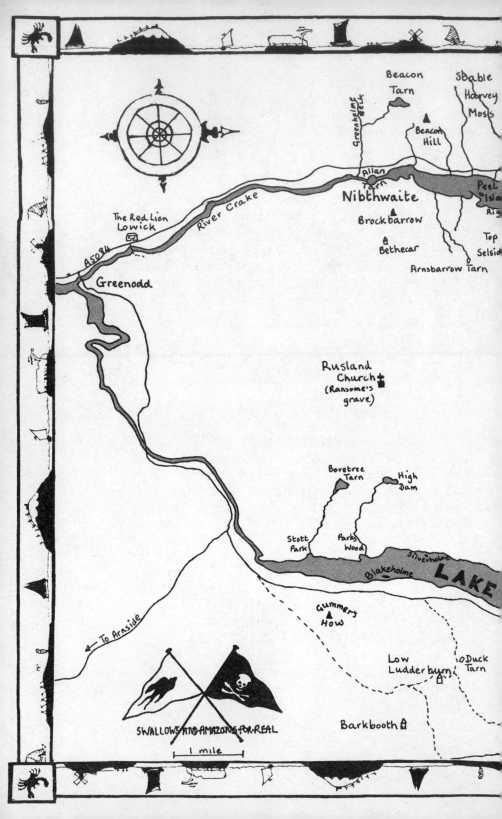

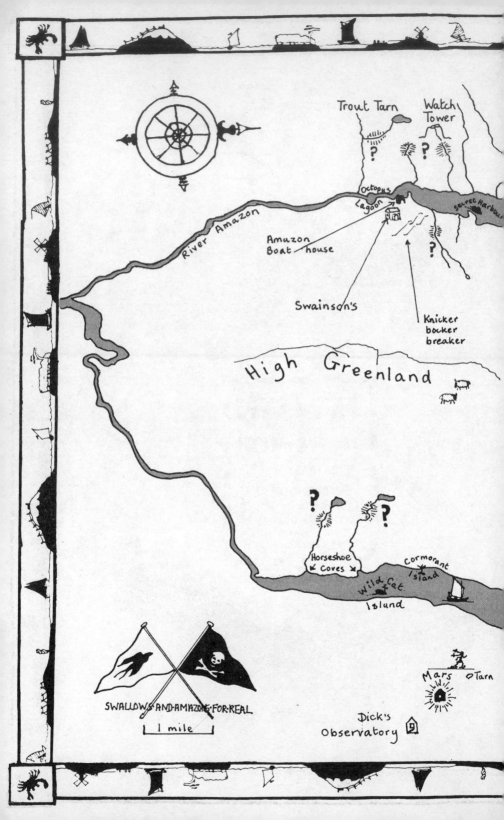

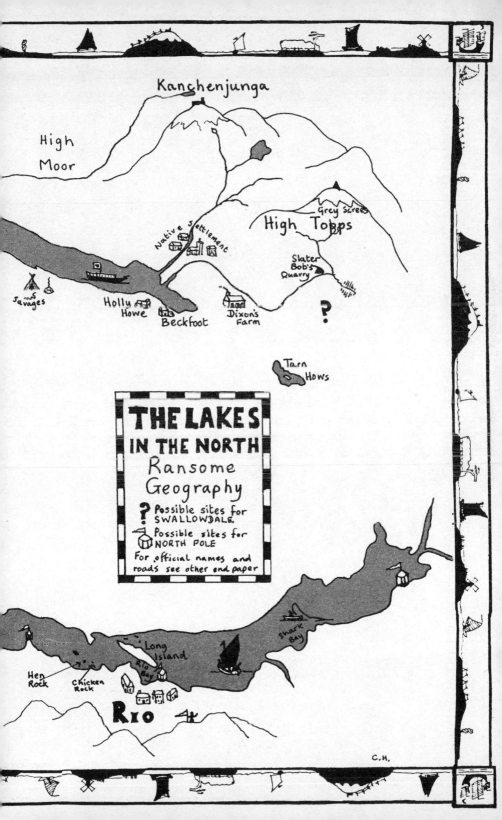

I

Into the Unknown

Three tents were pitched in the shelter of the sea wall. A kettle hissed on a camp-fire, and sausages pinioned on tent pegs spat fat into the flames. Four very muddy children sat round it, waiting hungrily for them to cook, listening to a story that was being read to them out of a fat green book. They were there and not there – the book was *Secret Water*, their camp was beside the real Secret Water. At any moment the Eels could leap over the dyke, the Amazons fire a green-feathered arrow at them, the Swallows file solemnly by, intent on their surveying. This was the last part of the children's quest. They had already looked down on a certain lake in the north in search of Wild Cat Island, and sailed along the rivers of the Norfolk Broads with *Coot Club* in mind. Now they were in the Walton Backwaters in Essex, recovering from crossing the Red Sea – or the Wade as the natives there call it.

Tilly, the oldest, liked Titty best. Daisy was quite happy with her Eely namesake. Ellen thought Bridget the nicest. Four-year-old Susanna was a little mystified by the whole undertaking, but made a splendid ship's baby. They were all cheerful allies in an adventure which had started when I read Hugh Brogan's excellent book, *The Life of Arthur Ransome*, and realized that we could actually go to the places which Ransome wrote about, and perhaps even meet some of his characters. It seemed that there had been a real family of five children: Taqui, Susan, Titty, Roger and Brigit. Would we

13

find other people who had appeared in the books? Was there really a Wild Cat Island and a Swallowdale? Could we climb Kanchenjunga? What were the Hullabaloos up to in the Broads today? Was there still a Mastodon splatching across the mud of Secret Water?

I had taken the first steps towards finding out some months earlier when I went to Leeds University. Most of Arthur Ransome's papers are kept there, in a pillared, oak-panelled room at the back of the Brotherton Library. There are piles of neat, dark-blue diaries, files of old letters dating back a hundred years or so, dozens of wallets of tiny black-and-white photographs temptingly labelled 'Lakes', 'Broads', 'Nancy Blackett', or more exotically 'Russia', 'Syria', and 'Lottie Blossom'. There is also a trunk, a substantial cabin trunk, with the remains of many labels on it, and the initials A. R. at one end. Any Ransome enthusiast would have guessed as I did that once upon a time it had been Captain Flint's trunk, the box stolen in *Swallows and Amazons* by the burglars from Bigland, and finally unearthed by Titty and Roger on Cormorant Island. Inside it in the story were Captain Flint's typewriter and the manuscript of *Mixed Moss*, by 'A Rolling Stone'. There is no sign of them now, but there are still 'a lot of diaries and old logs' which give vital clues to the truth behind the stories. In it too are blueprints for Ransome's own boats (*Racundra, Nancy Blackett, Peter Duck*), rolled-up maps, notebooks and sketches which all help to build up the picture of how Arthur Ransome wrote his books.

At first I hesitated. Would taking the books apart to see how they were constructed break their spell? When Ransome told an American visitor that his lake was based on not one but two (perhaps even three) lakes, he added that she should not tell her son, so that the boy could preserve his ideal image of a single lake. Perhaps he underestimated his readers. To judge from the urgent questions in the thousands of fan letters he received, they were hungry for real details. Even more to the point was the story he told to the same visitor a little later on. He had returned to the little harbour, a real

14

one, which in *Swallows and Amazons* his children enter using marks, or leading lights, and found that other children had placed actual marks where they had only existed before in the story. Far from breaking the spell, the discovery that so many of the children's adventures really happened to Ransome and his friends has made the magic stronger. Equally, the skill with which he wove together the real and the imaginary makes us understand what a truly great storyteller he was.

If this trunk was Captain Flint's trunk, then was Arthur Ransome Captain Flint? Both men were tall, fattish and balding at the time when Ransome settled down, at the age of forty-five, to write *Swallows and Amazons*. He was not quite a pirate, but he had had enough adventures to have earned a little peace beside the lake. The story of those adventures is told in his *Autobiography*. It might just as well have been called *Mixed Moss*, I decided, as I read first what Ransome had to say about himself, and then how he described Captain Flint in *Swallows and Amazons*:

> In the bay beyond the cape lay a strange-looking dark blue vessel. She was a long narrow craft with a high-raised cabin roof, and a row of glass windows along her side. Her bows were like the bows of an old-time clipper. Her stern was like that of a steamship. She had nothing that could properly be called a mast, though there was a little flagstaff, where a mast might have been, stepped just forward of the glass-windowed cabin. There was an awning over her after-deck, and under it a big fat man was sitting writing in a deck-chair . . .
>
> 'He's probably a retired pirate,' said Titty.
>
> Just then a harsh squawk sounded over the water, and a large green bird which they had not noticed shook itself where it stood perched on the rail that ran round the stern of the houseboat.
>
> 'He *is* a pirate,' said Roger. 'There's his parrot.'

It is true that Ransome was living in a cottage close to Lake

Windermere and not in a houseboat, but he knew that ship well. She was the *Gondola*, on near-by Coniston Water. When he wrote *Swallows and Amazons*, she was derelict. A few years later she was actually used as a houseboat, and today, by a kindly twist of fate, she is once more as she was originally designed to be, a passenger steamer making trips up and down the lake.

Ransome had a special reason for remembering her. When he was a small boy, his family used to spend long summer holidays at Swainson's farm, which was part of the tiny village of Nibthwaite at the southern tip of Coniston Water. In those days the *Gondola* was the best way of getting from one end of the five-mile-long lake to the other. The Captain was a particular friend of young Arthur's – he let him steer the ship occasionally, and used to toot farewell on his horn on the last journey of the season. Arthur named a high outcrop of rocks above Swainson's his own 'Gondola' and waved to the steamer from it. Other amusements which readers will recognize from the books were sliding down the steep rocks of the Knickerbockerbreaker (and being darned by Mrs Swainson, just like Roger in *Swallowdale*), fishing for minnows in the cut near the farm and for perch on the lake, climbing the famous local mountain, Coniston Old Man (Kanchenjunga in *Swallowdale*), exploring waterfalls and collecting caterpillars.

> Then, too, sometimes, when my father was fishing the lake for trout, he would row his whole family up to Peel Island where we landed in the lovely little harbour at the south end (that some who have read my books as children may recognise as borrowed for the sake of secrecy to improve an island in another lake). We spent the day as savages.

Arthur had two younger sisters and a younger brother. In 1896, when he was twelve, his family found other picnickers on the island, a well-known writer, William Collingwood, and his wife, who lived at the other end of the lake in a house

GERMAN AND AMERICAN VIEWS OF THE ATTACK ON THE
HOUSEBOAT, COMPARED WITH CLIFFORD WEBB'S
ORIGINAL ILLUSTRATION AND ARTHUR RANSOME'S OWN
DRAWING

called Lanehead. Were their two daughters, Dora and Barbara, then aged about eleven and ten, with them? If so, it is possible that the meeting gave him an idea for a much more exciting encounter in later years, when the Swallows charged the island camp to find, 'inside their own tents . . . two figures, kneeling, one with a bow ready to shoot, the other fitting an arrow'.

A few years later, when Ransome had chosen to be a writer rather than stay at university, he became very good friends with the Collingwoods. One of his favourite books was William Collingwood's story of a Viking boy discovering Coniston Water, *Thorstein of the Mere*. At the end of the book, Thorstein actually lived on Peel Island. Collingwood, an archaeologist, had found traces of a Viking dwelling there when he excavated it, so his story (like Ransome's own books) was based on reality.

Although Ransome was working in a small publisher's office in London, he dashed north whenever he could afford to do so, and sometimes stayed with the Collingwoods at Lanehead. He was given a room of his own to work in, and was met at Coniston pier by Dora and Barbara, who 'rowed *Swallow* over from the Lanehead boathouse, and helped me carry my things up the steep pathway to Lanehead'. It was a happy, casual household. While Mrs Collingwood painted Ransome sitting among the lupins, the girls worked with paint or clay in the 'Mausoleum', as they called their tumble-down conservatory, and Ransome studied the folk-tales that he hoped to retell some day. Barbara Collingwood made Arthur a bookplate for the library he was rapidly acquiring. She and Dora, with their brother Robin, taught him to sail in their dinghy *Swallow* (the first of many *Swallows* in Ransome's life) and in a larger boat, the *Jamrach*, which they borrowed from Miss Holt, at near-by Tent Lodge.

On other occasions, Ransome camped out in his tent, which he boasted was one of the first to be seen in the valley, using Low Yewdale farm (at the north end of Coniston Water) as a base. He also stayed much farther south, near the village of Cartmel, in a house called Wall Nook. He made friends with the charcoal-burners, who used to leave shiny black pipes for him at the Red Lion at Lowick. From gypsies he learnt strange folk-tales and the Romany skills of poaching and patterans. In London he met the poet John Masefield, author of *Salt-Water Ballads* and exciting tales of pirates on the Spanish Main. They walked to Greenwich and watched the tall ships slipping out to sea. Masefield wrote an article on sea shanties which Ransome arranged to publish. It includes most of the songs which appear in the books: 'Spanish Ladies', 'Hanging Johnny', 'Salt Beef', and so on.

Ransome's Bohemian life came to an end with his marriage to Ivy Walker in 1909, and a year later his only child, Tabitha, was born. Although he adored his little daughter, the marriage was not a happy one. Partly to escape it, he decided to go to Russia in 1913 and learn the language so that he could retell its folk-tales in English. He used Russian children's first reading books, graduating from 'the cat ate the rat' to 'the blue cat ate the purple rat' just as the young friends he made there were doing. His progress was faster than theirs; after a month he felt already as good at reading Russian as 'a rather backward child of ten', and very soon he spoke the language fluently.

He was in St Petersburg (now called Leningrad) when the First World War broke out. Unable to be a soldier because of his poor sight, and unable to find anything useful to do when he went back to England, he decided that the best contribution he could make would be to stay in Russia, reporting on the situation there for newspaper readers at home, as well as writing the book of fairy-stories published as *Old Peter's Russian Tales* in 1916. Although he hated politics, as his letters to his daughter Tabitha testified, Ransome was to witness the Russian Revolution at first hand. He played chess with its leader, Lenin (and beat him), and wrote extremely perceptive reports on the situation for the *Daily News*. He also met Evgenia Shelepina, secretary to another famous revolutionary, Trotsky, and she eventually became his second wife.

The story of how he crossed the lines of entrenched troops to rescue Evgenia from Moscow shows him as Captain Flint

3

BE FISHING OR PLAYING CATCH. POLITICS IS
WHAT KEEPS DOR-DOR IN RUSSIA AND MAKES
HIM SICK

MUMMUM WILL SAY THIS IS A
NAUGHTY DORDOR TO MAKE SUCH
A PICTURE.
BUT IT IS THE TRUTH AND
DORDOR DRAWS IT WITH HIS
WHOLE HEART.

HA! DORDOR HAS NOW BOUGHT A WHOLE
BOTTLE OF RED INK. HE SPILT
HALF IN OPENING IT BUT THERE
IS A LOT LEFT BESIDES A RED
SEA ON DORDORS PAPERS
ANY WAY THERE IS ENOUGH
TO MAKE MORE MESSES
WITH NEXT TIME.

at his best. Carrying his typewriter, and puffing at his pipe, he strolled casually through open country between the opposing armies. 'Nobody, I reasoned,' he wrote in his *Autobiography*, 'was going to shoot at a man walking slowly across and obviously enjoying his tobacco.' A line of riflemen stared in disbelief down the barrels of their weapons at the approaching figure. As Ransome reached the front line, a puzzled-looking platoon commander came up to him, waving a revolver.

'We have strict orders that anyone trying to cross the front is to be shot at once,' he told Ransome. 'Better get ready.'

Instead of panicking, Ransome suggested a cup of tea first, and then persuaded the officer that shooting him was a mistake which he could never put right, that he was a friend of Lenin's, and that it would be best to leave the decision to execute him to headquarters. He got away with his life, and then had to manage the even more difficult task of escaping from Moscow with Evgenia to the safety of the neutral Baltic states. Luckily, the young officer who raced up to shoot him on the way back turned out to be an old chess-playing friend. Instead of facing a firing squad, Ransome settled down at a chess-board to finish the game they had had to leave unsettled months before. Ransome tells the tale lightly enough. Less fortunate or resourceful travellers were summarily shot.

The next few years at Reval, on the Baltic Sea, made a sailor of him. First in *Slug*, then in *Kittiwake*, and finally in *Racundra*, he got to know the Baltic well enough to write a book, *Racundra's First Cruise*, which has been a favourite on sailors' bookshelves ever since. (There is more about these boats in Chapter VIII, 'Better Drowned than Duffers'.) Given better health, he would have written a second cruise book, but a chronically weak stomach meant that he suffered from ulcers, ruptures and other troubles for the rest of his life. He kept up his journalism for a few more years. The *Manchester Guardian* sent him to Moscow for Lenin's funeral, to Egypt after the assassination of the Sirdar, to the Sudan, to China, and again to Moscow in 1928. These were the years when the labels appeared on Captain Flint's Trunk.

Then came 1929, a year which he called 'a hinge year'. His doctor warned him that the strain of meeting newspaper deadlines could only make his stomach troubles worse. The *Manchester Guardian* offered him a tempting and well-paid job editing the weekly page of book reviews, and also asked him to go to Berlin. Money or his health? Ransome decided that it was time for a gamble. He handed in his resignation to the *Guardian*, and settled down seriously to a story which he had begun to write about some children – two girls and a boy

(Mary, aged twelve, Jane, thirteen, and Tom, three) who sailed a little boat called *Amazon*, and four other children (Dick, twelve, Susan, ten, Titty, eight, Roger, six, and a baby called Vicky 'who did not count') who sailed another little boat called *Swallow*. The first hesitant notes for the story are in a notebook, a 'Walker's Looseleaf Transfer Case'. With them is a pencil sketch of a lake, and a few names: Darien, Wild Cat Island, Holly Howe . . .

As we know, the gamble paid off. *Swallows and Amazons* and its sequels were to be every bit as successful as the legendary *Mixed Moss*, which, we are told in *Swallowdale*, was published in 1930, and went into an 8th edition in 1931. The pirate could retire in comfort, and enjoy more adventures with those young friends and some new ones. Eleven more books followed in what became a gigantic saga of over a million words. The stories were not necessarily to be linked at first. Dick and Dorothea only just avoided being replaced in *Coot Club* by two prim and proper children whom, thank goodness, Ransome never quite managed to create. It was only as he began the seventh, *We Didn't Mean to Go to Sea*, that he felt 'I knew pretty well by now what I wanted to do with these books, which were really each of them a single volume of one book.'

To jog memories of older readers, and to fill in any gaps, here is a list of all twelve of the books, with a brief sketch of their plots.

Swallows and Amazons (1930). John, Susan, Titty and Roger Walker set off in the sailing dinghy *Swallow* to camp on Wild Cat Island. There they make war and then peace with Nancy and Peggy Blackett, the Amazon pirates who live far down the lake at Beckfoot. During a night attack, Titty overhears burglars burying treasure on Cormorant Island. They make peace and then war with Captain Flint, find the trunk that is treasure only to him, and race home to Holly Howe with a fair wind and the promise of more to come.

Swallowdale (1931). The next summer, they camp on the island again. But John wrecks *Swallow* on Pike Rock near

A DRAWING BY CLIFFORD WEBB FROM THE FIRST EDITION
OF *SWALLOWS AND AMAZONS*

Horseshoe Cove, and the camp is transferred to the tiny valley
of Swallowdale. Hampered by a formidable great-aunt, Nancy
and Peggy and Captain Flint (their Uncle Jim) appear occasionally to feast, fish and make a new mast for *Swallow*. They
climb 'Kanchenjunga', get lost in the fog, and are saved by
charcoal-burners who mend Roger's broken ankle, and get

Titty a lift home on a tree-trunk. *Swallow* repaired, they all set up camp again on the island.

Peter Duck (1932). In the little green schooner *Wild Cat* (the island come to life) they sail to the Caribbean with the ancient mariner Peter Duck in search of treasure on Crab Island. The villainous crew of the *Viper* shadow them, but are cheated of their prey by a waterspout.

Winter Holiday (1933). The Ds, scientific Dick and romantic Dorothea, come for a winter holiday at Dixon's Farm. They signal to Mars (Holly Howe) and attract the attention of the Swallows and Amazons, who are staying there. Quarantine for mumps extends the holiday, and a full-scale polar expedition is launched from the icebound *Fram* (Captain Flint's houseboat).

Coot Club (1934). The Ds are introduced to the Norfolk Broads, the best nursery for sailors. They and the Admiral (Mrs Barrable) foil the attempts of the Hullabaloos to catch Tom Dudgeon, the boy who cast off the *Margoletta* to protect a coot's nest. Other allies are the identical sailing twins, Port and Starboard, and the cheerful local boys, the Death and Glories.

Pigeon Post (1936). Pigeons are the vital means of communication between the prospecting team of Swallows, Amazons and Ds and their base at Beckfoot. Their search for gold is made more difficult by the shady presence of Squashy Hat, who eventually turns out to be the long-awaited Timothy (but not an armadillo). Dowsing for water, collapsing mine shafts and a forest fire add to the excitement of the charcoal pudding and the discovery of a rich vein of copper in the hills.

We Didn't Mean to Go to Sea (1937). The Swallows drift out to sea, alone in a fog, on the seven-ton cutter *Goblin*, and get to Holland despite storms, steamers and seasickness – partly by good luck, but mainly by the extraordinarily good management of John, armed only with E.F. Knight's slim volume on sailing and his father's motto: 'Grab a chance and you won't be sorry for a might-have-been.'

Secret Water (1939). Commander Walker maroons the

Swallows on an island in Secret Water to map the unknown. They hunt a Mastodon and find the Amazons; give up Bridget as a human sacrifice and gain the friendship of a tribe of savage Eels – Daisy, Dum and Dee; cross the Red Sea and make corroboree. An elusive story, which slides away like an eel itself.

The Big Six (1940). A detective story in which Tom Dudgeon and the Ds work to clear the name of the Death and Glories, accused of casting off dozens of boats and stealing from the boat-builders.

Missee Lee (1941). The *Wild Cat* catches fire off the China coast, and Nancy meets a real she-pirate in the shape of Cambridge-educated Missee Lee. Roger's unexpected flair for Latin saves all their lives, and they escape via a little dragon and the graceful junk *Shining Moon*, leaving a sad Missee Lee to observe the duty a child owes a parent in true Confucian style.

The Picts and the Martyrs (1943). Great-aunt Maria surfaces again, but is totally routed by Captain Nancy's brilliant martyrdom. The Ds take cover in the woods as Picts, and learn housekeeping from local boy Jacky, who teaches them to tickle trout and provides rabbit to be skinned. Squashy Hat, now a friend, is in the background trying to get on with prospecting.

Great Northern? (1947). In a new ship, the Norwegian pilot boat *Sea Bear*, the Swallows, Amazons, Ds and Captain Flint sail around the Hebrides. Dick discovers a rare nesting pair of Great Northern Divers in the unfriendly territory of the Gaels. He makes the mistake of telling a ruthless egg-collector about them. They all spend the rest of the book trying to stop the egg-collector shooting them. On the last page the young Gael who has observed them with distant interest raises his hand in farewell – and so must we. It was the last book about them that Ransome completed.

The characters move with ease from book to book, chatting about earlier adventures, and even sending postcards to tell old friends who don't appear how they are getting on. Their time-scale is not that of the eighteen years which it took Ransome to write the books. The adventures all happen within about four. Bridget is a toddler in *Swallows and Amazons*, and just grown-up enough to be trusted to join the camp in *Secret Water*. A careful reading of the cross references from book to book makes them fit something like this:

Ransome Time

Year 1   Summer: *Swallows and Amazons*
           Winter: The story of *Peter Duck*
Year 2   Summer: *Swallowdale*
           Winter: *Winter Holiday*
Year 3   Easter: *Coot Club*
           Early Summer: *Pigeon Post*
           Midsummer: *We Didn't Mean to Go to Sea*
           Late Summer: *The Big Six*
                          Secret Water
           Winter: The story of *Missee Lee*
Year 4   Summer: *The Picts and the Martyrs*
           Late Summer: 'Coots in the North'
           Winter: The story of *Great Northern?*

Year three certainly looks a busy year, but by then there was a large cast of characters, and two adventures could be going on at the same time. *We Didn't Mean to Go to Sea* takes less than a week. 'Coots in the North' is the name which Hugh Brogan, Ransome's biographer, gave to the unfinished story which he found among uncatalogued Ransome papers at the Abbot Hall Museum in Kendal. On Ransome's death, his wife Evgenia gave his desk, his favourite books, and many other fascinating relics to Abbot Hall, and in the drawers of the desk Brogan came across the beginning of a story which ought to have told what happened after the great-aunt left in disarray at the end of *The Picts and the Martyrs*.

    Three of the books, *Peter Duck*, *Missee Lee* and *Great Northern?*, are different from the rest. In them the children are actually shot at with real guns. They are pure romance, realistic fantasy rather than fantastical reality. They are not set in the school holidays, but in a free time of their own;

they are stories told round the fire in winter. That meant that I would have no good excuse for going to investigate the Caribbean or China, or even the Hebrides. I could find the history behind them in the archives in Leeds. The rest of the books are set by the lakes of Cumbria, on the Norfolk Broads, near Ipswich in Suffolk and the Naze in Essex. Undoubtedly the best place to start exploring the real Ransome country was the Lake District, the country of Ransome's childhood and of much of his adult life, and the setting for five of the twelve stories.

II

Visiting Seal

'Every single place in those books exists somewhere,' Arthur Ransome wrote in 1937 to the magazine *Junior Bookshelf*. His letter was full of other clues to reassure me that the expedition which I had arranged to the Lake District, trying out my theories about Ransome geography, would not be a wild goose chase.

> The country is the country of my own childhood . . . for quite practical reasons, the place had to be disguised. So the Swallows and Amazons had a country of their own. Their lake is not altogether Windermere, though Rio is, of course, Bowness, because I had to take a great deal from Coniston. No island on Windermere had quite such a good harbour as that among the rocks where I first landed from a little boat I hardly like to say how many years ago. And a good many people have spotted that Kanchenjunga is the Old Man. But Cormorant Island is Silverholme on Windermere, and until a year or two ago the cormorants were there, and did a great deal of good by eating eels and thinning down the huge shoals of small perch. But now, alas, people have shot the cormorants and brought down the old tree on which they used to rest. Then, too, there has to be a little pulling about of rivers and roads, but every single place in those books exists somewhere and by now I know the geography of the country in my books so well that when I walk about in actual fact, sometimes it

seems to me that some giant or earthquake has been doing a little sceneshifting over night.

Like the surveyors of *Secret Water*, I was starting with a blank, official map. In two weeks' time, when the rest of the family arrived, I hoped to have added to it names like Darien, Holly Howe, the Octopus Lagoon, and Wild Cat Island. And Swallowdale, of course, although I had my doubts about the existence of such a perfect place.

I chose to come early in April, well before the holiday season, because I knew the Arthur Ransome atmosphere could hardly survive the hordes of visitors the lakes receive in summer. There is a real danger that they are being 'loved to death', as David Bellamy recently put it, by the twelve million people who now pass through every year. On March 31st, when I reached the road from Greenodd to Coniston, it was still as peaceful as it had been when the Ransomes made their slow holiday progress along it in John Swainson's farmcart and waggonette, after their railway journey from Leeds in the 1890s. There were no cars in those days.

'Up the winding hill and down again to Lowick Green' I drove just as they did, crossing the River Crake by Lowick Bridge and following a tiny road along the river to Nibthwaite itself. Cyril and Edith Ransome and their four children – Arthur, Joyce, Geoffrey and Cecily – would have got out here, to make it easier for the horses to pull the heavily laden carts up the steep slope to the farmhouse. I went on, to see the lake itself.

The road along the eastern edge ran through beech woods, not yet green, but bright with young moss and drifts of russet leaves. After some fields running down to the water, there were larch woods and a little shingle beach with the promising name of Low Peel Near. I looked up and down the lake, taking it in slowly. Hanging woods on the shores. White farmsteads set high on the hillsides. The huge snow-streaked bulk of the Old Man, Coniston's own mountain, far away to the north. Mile after mile of water, quite deserted, except for a few cabin yachts moored in sheltered bays. It is still as the Walker family first saw it, right at the beginning of *Swallows and Amazons*: 'With a lake as big as a small sea, a fourteen-foot dinghy with a brown sail waiting in the boathouse, and the little wooded island waiting for explorers, nothing but a sailing voyage of discovery seemed worth thinking about.'

I couldn't see Peel Island (my map showed that it was out of sight beyond the longer promontory of High Peel Near) and I did not have a dinghy. But strapped on the car's roof-rack was the next best thing, my windsurfer. Just then two sails shot out of a little bay opposite: not a brown one and a white one, but the rainbow wings of windsurfers, brilliant as tropical butterflies in the sunlight. It was irresistible. Forgetting that I had not yet found anywhere to stay, forgetting my sensible plan to drive round the whole lake, forgetting the gale warning I had heard on the car radio on the way up the M6, I unstrapped my board and rigged her sail. Squashing as many layers of clothes as possible under my wetsuit took some time, but at last I was on the water and away. I did not sail well. It is fatal when windsurfing to mind about falling in, and there was an icy snap to the wind and an edge to the water spraying up round my shins which told me that I would mind. I wobbled. My bottom stuck out. But a long beam reach took me safely across the lake, and I dropped my sail by the two other sailors. They were from Morecambe, where the sea had been so rough that they decided to come inland. One explained his caution by a back broken climbing mountains last October; he was just easing it into use again. The other just happily fell in and climbed out again with true beginner's grit.

Just as I was gaining confidence, a terrific gust of wind came snorting down the lake, darkening the water menacingly, and whipping the boom out of my hands. I looked at my huge regatta sail and remembered John's failure to reef in *Swallowdale*, and the resulting shipwreck on Pike Rock. The gust passed. I pulled up the sail and began to relax, buzzing to and fro and enjoying the feeling of being at last on 'the lake in the north' (or at least on the Coniston part of it). It felt curiously familiar. Thin and flat as Ransome's drawings are, they catch the mood of the countryside extraordinarily accurately.

Another blast of wind from the other end of the lake caught me unawares, and I went half-in. I had been right about the water being cold. I began to tack back up the lake to Low Peel Near. The waves were now white-capped, rearing up to fight back the board's progress. Watching the boathouses along the shore, I realized how little headway I had made. No wonder Nancy and Peggy had been so late for supper at Beckfoot, far down at the other end of the lake, when the wind was against them. A third tornado sent me in, head and all, right under the sail. As I sank, I remembered what Arthur Ransome used to do whenever he came back to Coniston Water: 'I had a private rite to perform. Without letting the others know what I was doing, I had to dip my hand in the water, as a greeting to the beloved lake or as a proof to myself that I was home.'

Feeling that enough tribute had been paid, I gave up the unequal struggle against the wind, trolled to the nearest shore, and left the windsurfer there. As I walked back along the road to the car, a dripping Amazon in black neoprene and orange buoyancy harness, staid heads turned in passing saloons. I changed in the scanty shelter of my hatchback, got thankfully behind the wheel, and drove back to the board. As I was rolling up her sail, the mountaineering mariner came over. He pointed to the storm sail on his own mast, and gave me some useful advice on lake sailing. He said nothing, I reflected later, that I could not have learnt from the Ransome books on the back seat of the car.

The lakeshore road wound north past woods, beaches, and rocky points. Suddenly I saw Peel Island, its steep sides dropping into the lake, a topknot of trees crowning it, and the straggling rocks of the harbour which Ransome borrowed for Wild Cat Island stretching southwards. It was not Wild Cat Island itself, but it was (and still is) a very special place for several generations of Collingwoods. 'With an island like that, who could be content to live on the mainland

and sleep in a bed at night?' the Swallows had asked. Arthur Ransome had camped on it more than once as a young man. I considered. There was a hammock and a sleeping-bag in the back of the car. With those, a billycan and matches from Coniston village I could do the same. It might mean two or three voyages taking supplies across, but the sun was shining encouragingly and the lake looked almost calm. Then I saw a noticeboard at the end of the island, and foolishly read it through my binoculars:

> *National Trust*
> No Fires
> No Camping
> Please take your litter home

Like Missee Lee, I let personal inclination wrestle with duty, and lost. Still, there was some compensation. I knew that a little farther along the lakeside was Bank Ground Farm, a house which can reasonably claim to be the original of Holly Howe. Ransome took Clifford Webb, the first illustrator of his books, along there to draw Roger tacking up the field towards it. Today Mrs Lucy Batty offers bed and breakfast to visitors, and once upon a time it was the holiday home of the children who gave their names and, I think, a little of themselves to the Walker family.

Dora, the oldest of the Collingwood girls, married a schoolfriend of her brother Robin's called Ernest Altounyan. They had five children, Taqui, Susan, Titty, Roger and Brigit, and lived in Syria. About every four or five years they came back to Coniston Water to see their grandparents at Lanehead, and they usually stayed at Bank Ground Farm close by. It shared the Lanehead boathouses, and had a steep field down to the shore.

In the summer of 1928, Ernest Altounyan bought two stout sea-going sailing dinghies, fourteen-footers originally made at Crossfield's boatyard at Arnside. They were christened *Swallow*, after the old Collingwood dinghy that Ransome and the Collingwood children had sailed many years earlier, and *Mavis* (which means song thrush, as well as being

1 *Above left:* Captain Flint's pirate past: Arthur Ransome in Russia in 1918.
2 *Above right:* Dora and Barbara Collingwood taught Ransome to sail.
3 Lanehead on Coniston Water, the family home of the Collingwoods. Was this the model for Beckfoot?

4 *Left:* the real Swallows: Susan, Taqui, Titty (sitting) and Roger Altounyan in 1926.

5-7 *Below:* the Altounyans sailing on a lake in Syria, with (*inset*) details from portraits by their mother Dora – Taqui (*left*) looking her most Captain Nancyish, and Titty the dreamer.

8 *Opposite:* Georgina and Pauline Rawdon-Smith. Were they Nancy and Peggy?

9 *Below* Ransome sailing *Swallow* across Rio Bay (Bowness-on-Windermere).

10-11 *Top:* Blakeholme on Windermere was the island most used as Wild Cat Island. In the foreground is Silverholme (Cormorant Island) and a film version of Titty mooring her prize, *Amazon*, just where she should. *Above:* Ransome at work in the barn at Low Ludderburn.

Titty's real name). Ransome and Altounyan thoroughly enjoyed teaching the children to sail on the very lake where they themselves had learnt. Taqui and Titty usually sailed *Mavis*, and Susan and Roger *Swallow*, while their father and their honorary Uncle Arthur yelled 'Duffers!' at them from the stone jetty by the boathouses.

When *Swallows and Amazons* was published two years later, its dedication read: 'To the Six for whom it was written in exchange for a pair of slippers'. In the collection of Ransome's papers at Leeds I found the draft of an open 'letter to a friend' which explained why. It also spelt out the connection between those children and the children in the books.

Swallows and Amazons
A letter to a friend

My dear . . . .

Yes. It is perfectly true that *Swallows and Amazons* was written in exchange for a pair of slippers. But I ought to make it plain that the Walkers had no sort of idea that they were making an exchange when they gave me the slippers. They gave me the slippers as a birthday present, free, gratis and for nothing, and I mentioned the slippers in the dedication only because I hoped that it might occur to them that perhaps sometime or other I should like another pair. They are very good slippers you know, real Turks, bright scarlet, shaped like barges. You can't get such slippers at home. At least I can't up here in the hills.

The slippers, I say, were given to me as a present by the Walkers just before they went away to . . . Syria. It was just that present that put it into my head that it would be rather fun to write a book to send after them to remind them of home. But the book might have been any sort of book if it had not been for one of the two small boats that come into the story. You see, for a whole summer the Walkers had been sailing the *Swallow*, the little boat you found me sailing last summer, the one with the brown sail. She had become, in a way, in the most natural of ways, their boat. They had sailed her and sailed her until for each one of them she was a member of the family. There were several other small boats about (one of which appears in the book as the *Amazon*) but not one that made herself so beloved as *Swallow*. She was a very small sailing boat, built for sailing on the estuary, a fast little boat and a steady little boat, in fact the best little boat that ever was built. And the Walkers had sailed her for a season and now were off to the East, and now I should be sailing her while the Walkers would be looking at camels and trying to keep the dust out of their eyes and mosquitoes the right side of the curtains. Obviously the thing to do was to write them a book all about the little *Swallow* they were leaving behind.

I said nothing about it, because I wasn't so sure that I could do it. Wanting to write a book is not at all the same thing as getting it written. So I said nothing about it, and the Walkers left the lake and hills and disappeared altogether, except for very rare letters with blue stamps on them with pictures of hills in the desert. And I went sailing on the lake in *Swallow*, thinking of the sailing I had had with the Walkers and remembering the lake years and years ago before they were born, when I used to play about on it with their mother and father who were then not much bigger than the Walkers are now. I sailed and I fished and I landed on islands and made my tea and sailed again and I thought of a camp of years ago on the best of islands that you and I know well. And it occurred to me that to do the thing properly I should have to put the Walkers in the story as well as their boat, and then I remembered the Blacketts. The wind dropped early that day and I was a long time sailing home. But before I got home I had the beginning of the book in my head and I took a sheet of paper and began to put down the things that happened.

But as soon as I began to write the programme went to pieces. I found that the Walkers and the Blacketts whom I was putting into the story cared not twopence about my paper programme for them but went ahead with the story in their own way. They kept doing things that had not been allowed for in the Contents. It was as if all I had to do was to play kettledrum tunes on the typewriter and see what words came out at the top. It was as if Able-seaman Titty and Mate Susan and Captain John and Roger the Ship's Boy were pulling my fingers this way and that. It was their affair, not mine.

Meanwhile the Walkers away out there in Syria had found a sheet of water and got a boat sent out to them and were sailing themselves. They wrote and told me about it, and how they smashed a rudder and lost a mast and how the boat leaked like a sieve and all the rest of it. They even sent me a photograph. Here it is. A photograph of them sailing their new boat somewhere near Antioch. After that, of course, I ought to have thought that there was no need to go on writing *Swallows and Amazons*. But I could not stop. I used to hate everything else I had to do (except fishing and sailing) and I used to get away into my room in the top of the old barn (putting cement to keep the rain out drove the owls away, but you'll be glad to hear they went no further than the yew trees, and one of them, calling at night, made his contribution to the book). Up in the old barn I used to wonder what was going to happen and how, and while I was writing things came tapping out on the paper that used to make me get up and walk about and chuckle as if someone were telling me a story instead of me writing one for other people. Even when I had to do other things, I used to feel happier just to have the box in which the manuscript was piling up somewhere within sight, so that I could remember that I should soon be able to go off with the rest of the crew and have some more adventures. Lots of things happened that didn't go into the book. The book was meant to be a very little one. It grew and grew until it was over 350 pages and I had to bring it to an end by main force. Which I did, and have been wanting to start another ever since.

ARTHUR RANSOME

So the book was written *for* the Altounyan children. It used their names, but it was not necessarily *about* them. It was about *Swallow* and *Mavis/Amazon* and a collection of children of their ages. That having been said, it is clear from the family's reception of *Swallows and Amazons* that there were some near likenesses. Everyone agreed that the famous 'Better Drowned than Duffers' telegram was exactly in Ernest Altounyan's style. He was a frequent telegram sender, and always made them terse and witty. He was also a fanatically keen sailor, and quite capable of marooning his entire family in Secret Water. Dora rather resented her Australian ancestry (Ransome had borrowed that from his own grandfather, whom he recalled skipping nimbly out of the way of a boomerang that returned faster than he had expected) but in other respects she was 'the best of all natives', painting away happily while her children led remarkably independent lives.

Roger Altounyan became an eminent doctor, famous for his discovery of the Intal asthma treatment. I asked him about his past as a ship's boy, and found that he still relished the memory of it. He felt that Ransome was extraordinarily accurate in his characterization of the brothers and sisters. As a child Roger was fascinated by the way technical things like engines worked. Later he preferred his boats without motors, especially when on the lake. He told me that Taqui certainly had been tomboyish, and loved sailing, swimming and rowing. And it was Susie who thought most about whether they were warm enough and ate properly. Titty, he emphasized, was the most literate and original of them all. She read very fast and widely at an age when he could hardly get through a page or two.

'So that was why you didn't take a book to Wild Cat Island when the rest did?' I asked, when I talked to him.

'Absolutely. I still find it quite a struggle to read! I love fishing, though.'

I remembered the incident that led to the naming of Shark Bay in *Swallows and Amazons*:

'Where's your float, Roger?' said the mate.

'And look at your rod,' said Titty.

Roger jumped up and caught hold of his jerking rod, which he had put down while he was counting the catch. He felt a fish at the end of his line. Just as he was bringing it to the top there was a great swirl in the water, and his rod was suddenly pulled down again. Roger hung on as hard as he could, and his rod was bent almost in a circle.

'It's a shark! It's a shark!' he shouted.

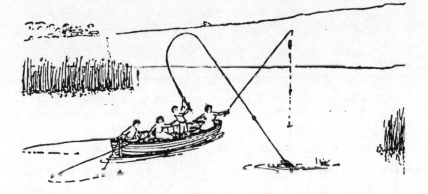

The real Roger went on to tell me that, soon after *Swallows and Amazons* had been published, he had actually caught a pike on the lake.

'I was only about seven, and on my own in *Mavis*. It was getting dark when I hooked it, and easily the worst part was being all alone in the boat with it after I had got it aboard. It was very frightening.'

The experience did not put him off fishing. He told me he still used *Mavis* for fishing on Coniston Water, his children joining him there for family holidays, windsurfing, fishing and sailing. The latest addition to the family, his four-week-old granddaughter, had already been taken up to the top of the Old Man, and out to Peel Island for a picnic. I asked him what he had seen of the Ransomes after the summer when he learnt to sail.

'Not very much. I went to stay with them near Ipswich

the year the king [George V] died, and I remember Evgenia putting me straight into a bath and scrubbing me from top to toe. I suppose like all small boys after a term at school I must have been very dirty. They were always great fun to be with, full of humour and very generous. Evgenia was an excellent cook.'

Roger found the accuracy with which Ransome had predicted the way they grew up almost uncanny.

'How could he have known, for example, that we would be left by our parents to fend for ourselves so much? We used to spend the school holidays at Lanehead with nobody there but the Cook, and even Taqui was only fourteen or fifteen at the time. It was certainly a case of better drowned than duffers.'

Roger's parting remark showed that he was more than a character dancing at its author's bidding: 'The one thing I'm proud of is something that Uncle Arthur always wanted to do but never quite managed, fishing for char under sail. His line used to get tangled, or he'd find himself sailing too fast or too slow. But I've been experimenting, and I've got it down to a fine art now. I've caught quite a few.'

What about Mate Susan? Susie Altounyan, who now lives with her family in France, was less happy about her fictional personality. She hated the pall of respectability which the Susan of the books wished upon her. Looked at from the author's point of view, Susan has to be a mini-grown-up, because only with such a child in charge would it be reasonable for parents to let their children be so independent. This is spelt out in *Swallowdale*:

She never allowed excitements such as sleeping in the open half-way up a mountain, or a naval battle, or a dangerous bit of exploring, to interfere with the things that really matter, such as seeing that water is really boiling before making tea with it, having breakfast at the proper time, washing as usual, and drying anything that may be damp. Really, if it had not been for Susan, half the Swallows' adventures would have been impossible, but, with a mate as good as that, to see that everything went as it should, there was no need for any native to worry about what was happening.

Susie Altounyan's own theory is that Susan Walker owed a good deal to Ransome's wife Evgenia, 'the whistle-blowing mate' as she was called by youngsters who sailed with them later. Certainly, shopping lists and 101 different ways of cooking fish were Evgenia's trademarks. Her cool-headed behaviour when sailing through a nasty gale in *Racundra* compares well with Susan's on *Goblin*, once her initial panic and seasickness are over. *Racundra*'s mainsail had been lost, she had no sidelights, and she was careering through steep seas in pitchdark night.

> The Cook struggled up the companionway with a sandwich. She asked, with real inquiry, 'Are we going to be drowned before morning?'
> I leaned forward from the steering-well and shouted, 'Why?'
> 'Because I have two Thermos flasks full of hot coffee. If we are, we may as well drink them both. If not, I'll keep one till tomorrow.'

Susie's letters to me showed that she still remembered the Ransomes with affection.

> I must have been at least six by the time we first saw Arthur Ransome, but we heard a lot about him and his fishing and sailing exploits from our parents. When I say that we were also brought up on Beatrix Potter, you will easily see how Jeremy Fisher and Arthur Ransome got completely mixed up, with their fishing tackle, worms and basket, etc. In fact, when we met him at Low Ludderburn, which was so small, the comparison still held good!

The next time they met was in 1928, the year of *Swallow* and *Mavis*, and of sailing lessons on Coniston Water.

He was a great friend of our parents and we mutually adopted one another. He undertook to teach us to 'fish' and generally behave un-tripperishly in a sailing boat. All hullabaloo instincts were stamped out of us from the very start! Uncle Arthur's wrath was as explosive as his mirth and very startling to small girls, but we soon learnt to avoid it by immediate execution of orders from the man at the tiller . . .

Expeditions with the Ransomes were always exciting and full of laughter, and Aunt Evgenia was as generous to us children as her bosom, which was in keeping with her deep voice!! Copious meals cooked by her were taken in the tiny dining-room at Low Ludderburn where we came, for the first time in our lives, face to face with a huge pike in a glass case, one of AR's trophies, displayed on the mantelpiece.

We were often allowed up in the barn, where we were told the famous Anansi stories over and over again until poor Uncle Arthur would refuse from sheer exhaustion to tell us another . . .

'Were you really the Swallows?' people used to ask us. We always answered: 'Yes, but we never did any of the things in the book; it's what we should like to have done.'

Before setting off for the lakes, I met Taqui in London. Ransome had made the oldest Swallow a boy, Captain John, for the obvious reason that he wanted the book to appeal to as many people as possible. Roger had said that Taqui was a tomboy as a girl, but that didn't mean she was like Captain John, who is really the competent boy that Ransome wished he himself had been. The person who instantly springs to mind on seeing the portrait of Taqui painted by her mother when she was about thirteen is Captain Nancy. I remembered that it had been Taqui and Titty who sailed *Mavis*, the original *Amazon*. I even found a letter which seemed to bear out my theory. It was sent to Ransome by Taqui from Syria when she was fifteen. She had been teaching some lubberly Americans to sail, and described with glee how one of them stood with his legs astride the tiller. The letter ended up, 'Anyway, I enjoyed giving orders and being thoroughly Captain Nancyish.'

Today, still as sparkling and energetic as the early portrait showed her, Taqui is a writer. She told me that she went on sailing enthusiastically after those early lessons. Once she had passed the family test of jumping into the lake fully dressed ('I still remember the checked pink Viyella of the blouse and skirt I wore to do it') she could take the helm herself. In Syria they sailed dinghies on the lake at Antioch, and in later years she and Titty joined the Ransomes for a sailing holiday on the Broads. Taqui went cruising in his boat the *Nancy Blackett* several times, and once Ransome arranged for her to crew for a friend of his who was sailing to Holland (to take photographs which would be used for the drawings for *We Didn't Mean to Go to Sea*). He also helped her join the Cruising Association.

Other odd flashes of the past came to her: the baler kept in the back of Trojan (Ransome's huge car and probably the original Rattletrap) for seasick passengers, the 'zestful' way Uncle Arthur talked to them, and his patient explanation of fishing techniques. She recalled the 150 perch he and Evgenia had caught in one day on Coniston Water and made into soup; a sharp contrast to the occasional fish the Altounyan children managed to hook, grill lovingly with bacon, and share between the four of them. Most vivid of all were her memories of Peel Island. Here is a description of a visit to it, from the book she wrote about her childhood, *In Aleppo Once*:

Roger always fetched the boat out. There were cobwebs everywhere in the dark boathouse, especially on the shoulders of tweed jackets; there were forgotten jamjars and minnow traps, tins, old oars and sails all covered with cobwebs. From the gloom we glide out into the sunshine. Worth putting up sail? Yes, I think so. The flash of minnows darting away, perhaps even a striped perch. The brown sail hoisted, arguments about who is to sit where, who is to sail, and where the bundles are to be put. We are off. Peel Island is about four miles down the lake, so with an off-shore wind we get there in about an hour and a half. The landmarks slip by one by one: steamer pier, Ruskin's pier, Mr Talbot's boathouse, Brantwood, Fir Island – we are halfway. After Fir Island, Peel Island is always suddenly near. Like a green tuffet, sitting in the water, the trees covering the rocks. Submerged rocks like great brown fish under the water and we think we know where we are, but sometimes there is a scrape, the centreboard jumps and a scale of white and orange paint appears, visible on the rock when the water is clear . . .

[They gathered wood, lit a fire.]

The kettle begins to boil; one or two tiny bubbles at first and then the spout dribbles all over the ashes with a hiss and tea is ready. After tea the wind drops with the sun and fishing begins out on the end of the rocky point. The perch at Peel Island are always extra big. The wind drops gradually, soon there is very little sound or movement except the plop of fish jumping for flies, and sometimes the raucous shriek of the line being paid out, or the giant splash of someone diving in for a swim. If it is still fine we decide to spend the night there – or row home in the dark.

Later on, I would meet Titty and Brigit, who both live on the shores of Coniston Water, but I knew that this tempting game of pinning real people to the characters could not be taken too far. Even if Ransome did say that he had found 'Titty and Roger most comically like their imaginary selves' when he met them two years later in Syria, there is still a world of difference between the initial model and the fully developed character, whose only real existence is in the mind of the author.

With places I was (I thought then) on safer ground. 'Every single place exists', Ransome had said, 'somewhere.' And here I was at the Altounyans' summer holiday home, Bank Ground Farm, or Holly Howe. It is a rambling, L-shaped house, with barns beside it, and low-ceilinged, friendly rooms.

Luckily two of a party of campers had cancelled their book-
ing, and Mrs Batty had a spare bed. After a welcome hot
bath and a huge helping of gammon, I sat in the square
windowbay in the corner of the dining-room with a pot
of tea. The window faced north-west, commanding the lake
like the bridge of a ship. In the film version of *Swallows and
Amazons*, Virginia McKenna had sat in this window at a writing desk being Mrs Walker, watching Roger tacking up the
field from the Peak of Darien.

Before the sun set, I went down to the shore. There was no
Darien there, no pine woods, no promontory dropping like a
cliff into the lake. But I knew where it was. I had found
a postcard in Leeds carefully marked up by Ransome for
Clifford Webb to draw from: Friar's Crag, on Derwent
Water. Ironically, the film had used exactly that location for
the Darien in their film, without the slightest idea that they
were quite right to be doing so. They must have been
instinctive Ransomites.

Beside the three stone boathouses and the little jetty I
found two white hulls upside down on the shore. I could
have guessed their names: *Swallow*, *Amazon*. Out on the lake
a red-sailed Mirror dinghy was struggling gamely up against
the wind. Far away at the very foot of the lake was a white
sail. Perfect. But what would it be like in high summer?
Squadrons of *Swallows* laying alongside flotillas of *Amazons*
and giving battle? At the moment it looked as if nothing
could spoil Coniston Water's tranquillity. The friendly windsurfer with the storm sail had told me that no motor boats
were allowed on this lake, which is kept sacred to sailing and
fishing. By contrast, thousands of power boats are licensed to
sail on Windermere. 'I'd give you half an hour at the most
there before you were knocked down on a windsurfer,' he
had said. 'If it wasn't by a waterskier, it would be by the ferry
or a steamer.' I hoped he was being pessimistic, for Windermere was my next port of call.

After a very comfortable night and a greedy breakfast, I
left Bank Ground Farm. Its visitors' book was packed with
enthusiastic comments from the children who still spend

their holidays there, so the Battys must be worthy successors to the Jacksons of Holly Howe. I stopped the car at the top of their track and went to look at the large white house a little higher on the hillside. It was Lanehead, the Collingwoods' old home, where Ransome had sat among the lupins and written his first fairy-stories, and from which he used to sail down the lake to Peel Island to camp with his friends. Today it has the cold vacant face of an institution. It is an outdoor pursuits centre, with a rack of fibreglass canoes where the conservatory once was. Yet to my mind it was important: was it the model for Beckfoot?

Lots of things were wrong with my theory. Beckfoot should have been on the other side of the lake, in the shadow of Kanchenjunga. It should have the river winding past it, and Octopus Lagoon beside it. This house did not even look very like the drawings of Beckfoot (the best are in *The Picts and the Martyrs*). On the other hand, there was nowhere on the opposite side of the lake which fitted the description of Beckfoot, and I suspected that the Octopus Lagoon was far away at the foot of the lake in Nibthwaite. It was Taqui and Roger who had started me thinking along these lines. They had both mentioned the school holidays they used to spend alone at Lanehead after their grandparents had died. If no relations were around, the Cook, Ada Birkett from Tilber-thwaite, used to look after them, and occasionally friends of their parents, honorary uncles, had dropped in for a few days to keep an eye on them. I thought of Nancy and Peggy alone in Beckfoot in *The Picts and the Martyrs*. A generation earlier, Ransome had had a study there, just as the Blacketts' Uncle Jim did, and I remembered Dora and Barbara rowing over to meet him at Coniston, just as the Amazons collect Dick and Dorothea from Rio. Like Beckfoot, Lanehead was a real house, not a holiday home for visitors. Other places might be better placed geographically, but Lanehead and its history *felt* right for Beckfoot.

III

Signalling to Mars

Lake Windermere, twice as long and twice as wide as Coniston Water, felt more like an ocean than a small sea. To see it, I had scrambled up a hill called Gummer's How (1,054 ft) down at the south-eastern end of the lake. The view was uncannily like the endpaper map of *Swallows and Amazons*. Far below lay bays, headlands, sedate houses with well-kept lawns running down to the water's edge, and the River Leven winding its way from the foot of the lake to the sea. The northern end, 'unexplored ARCTIC', was invisible, just as it is on the book's map. The islands dotted over it were perfect. Enormous Belle Isle (the Swallows' Long Island) curled away from Bowness (or Rio). Round it, lesser islands echoed the pattern on the map, right down to the tiny Hen and Chicken rocks. Much closer to me were Blakeholme and Silverholme, already familiar from a letter Ransome wrote to a friend who was planning to sail on Windermere:

Oh yes, I meant to tell you about Blakeholme. This is one of the best islands . . . It is no longer safe as it used to be to sail between Blakeholme and the shore. The way to the landing place is now to sail past the island on the outer side, and then giving good clearance to the submerged rocks at the south end, to come round it and up the inside FROM THE SOUTH, when you will find a delightful little landing place of fine shingle, and a very good place for a camp. This was the island most used as Wild Cat Island,

45

and you will see Cormorant Island from it (proper name, Silverholme) with the bare tree and nearly always the cormorants, six of them, perched on the boughs or fishing.

Once the Altounyan family had gone back to Syria, Ransome had *Swallow* brought to a Bowness boatyard. So it was while sailing on Windermere, landing on its islands to make tea, fishing in its bays, that he thought out the story of *Swallows and Amazons.* As a small boy, he had gone to school in Windermere town. He had tickled trout in the becks that ran down to it, and skated on the frozen ice of Bowness Bay in the icy winter of 1895 when the whole lake froze. He wrote the book while living at Low Ludderburn, just to the east of the lake.

His diary entries reveal his favourite Windermere places during those months. He mentions the bay by Storr's Hall as a good place to moor. Geographically it would be about right for Houseboat Bay. The point there sticks out into the lake just as Darien did, but I could see from Gummer's How that it was not steep enough for Titty's Peak. The little six-sided temple on its tip might have made a passable North Pole for *Winter Holiday*, if well banked up with snow. At the very north end of the lake is the Wateredge Hotel, where the Ransomes used to moor and take tea in the garden looking down the lake. I had stopped there on the way to Gummer's How and done the same, looking hopefully for better North Poles, but not seeing any. White Cross Bay, a little farther south, is mentioned as a good place to fish, and Ransome caught a fine pike there, so it could have been Shark Bay.

What about Swallowdale? It ought to be almost exactly west of Gummer's How, on the opposite side of the lake. I could see two good Horseshoe coves. One belonged to a large house, with newly built holiday apartments in it, the other was more promisingly occupied by some green tents. Streams ran down through steep woods to both bays, and from my map I could see two or three small tarns in the moorland above. But, of course, there could be no trekking from there to Kanchenjunga, the mountain which Ransome had definitely identified as the Old Man near Coniston Water. It began to look as if the *lake* of the books was almost exactly Windermere, but that the *land* round about it was much more like Coniston.

I decided to take a closer look at Blakeholme and Silverholme. There are two public launching sites, one at Fellfoot and one at Bellman's Landing by Storr's Point. Both would have meant a sail of over a mile to reach the islands, pleasant enough in the summer, but more than I relished on a cold spring day. Thanks to some obliging woodmen, I found a much closer but strictly unofficial take-off point. The sun was still shining, and the wind was coming down the lake fast, though less gustily than it had been on Coniston. First I windsurfed to Blakeholme, rounding the southern point and coming up on the little landing place that Ransome recommended.

It is an excellent island, about 150 yards long and seventy or so wide. I found a clearing in the centre, with plenty of room for tents and a camp-fire and enough cover for Titty to have escaped the Amazons on the memorable night she captured their ship. There is nothing quite like the lone pine lookout, although the island is well wooded. Other trees might have caught up with that single one in fifty years, or perhaps the tree itself has fallen. The only serious things wrong with Blakeholme are its lack of a secret harbour (which we know was borrowed from Peel Island) and its closeness to the shore. There is no room at all for Shark Bay; in fact it would be easy to swim – perhaps even wade – to it from the Hill of Oaks Caravan Park on the lakeshore beside it.

From the landing place on Blakeholme I windsurfed right across the broad expanse of Windermere to Silverholme, about half a mile north-west. Its position is exactly right for Titty to have happened on it in *Amazon* when she was making for the opposite shore from Blakeholme/Wild Cat Island. It doesn't matter that it is close to the shore, because it was meant to be. Again, it would be simple to wade out to it from the lakeshore path, which begins just after the YMCA centre on the west side of the lake. I fastened my windsurfer's uphaul under a large flat rock with some care, not liking the idea of her reaching Rio alone and leaving me marooned. Then I went ashore, and paced out the island. It was rather larger than I had expected, about forty yards or so long, but it had just the profile of Ransome's drawings: flat central rocks and loose stones all around. The cormorants have gone, and there are several good-sized trees on it, so it no longer has the feeling of a desert island. Right in the middle of it, however, was something which made it unarguably Cormorant Island – the huge toppled stump of an ancient tree, weathered and burnt and hacked at, but still there. I could hear the able-seaman saying to the boy Roger that they would need a good big flat stone to go at the back of their fireplace, as she pulled at one wedged into the roots of the fallen tree.

> It moved easily, and as it did so, all thoughts of making fireplaces flew out of Titty's mind.
> 'Help, Roger,' she shouted. 'Where's the pickaxe?' . . .
> 'We've found it, we've found it, we've found it,' shouted Titty. She pulled the stone right away to one side, and there was a torn label on the corner of the box, a label with a picture of a camel and a pyramid, and the word Cairo, plain in big letters.

The wind was freshening. I unhooked the uphaul, and sailed off again, this time to have a closer look at Storr's Head. It was wooded, but, as I had thought, too flat for Darien, although from it there was a fine view of Blakeholme, enticingly distant to the would-be mariners.

I returned to the eastern shore, unrigged the board, and asked the friendly woodmen what the islands were like in the summer. They told me that lots of people played about on them, swimming there, or landing from boats. Today, there was not another soul to be seen, nor were there any signs of litter or destruction. And as far as I could see, there were no noticeboards. If it was as fine as this when my own children came to join me, we could hire a boat in Bowness and picnic there, or even camp.

For the moment, I left the lake and drove past Gummer's How to the Winster valley. I was going to stay there for the next three weeks in a cottage owned by some kind relations with a weakness for Arthur Ransome. They gave me an excellent lunch, showed me how to keep from freezing or starving to death, and then left for their home in Sheffield. I unpacked, pushed the long dining table into the great south-facing window, and spread it with books, papers and typewriter. Only two miles down the valley was Low Ludderburn, the house where Ransome had written the first five stories, sitting at his own great south-facing window in the barn. I would be looking out at his real world, and trying to see into that of the stories. I felt like Dick and Dorothea in *Winter Holiday* when they peer longingly through their telescope at Holly Howe from the old barn high on the hill behind Dixon's and watch the heads hanging out of the top window of the white-painted end wall.

'What's the good of thinking about them?' said Dorothea. 'They might as well be in some different world.'

Dick started so sharply that he almost dropped his telescope.

'Why not? Why not?' he said. 'All the better. Just wait till dark and we can try signalling to Mars.'

The signalling system which the Swallows and Amazons and Ds eventually developed, with its square and triangle hoisted at different angles and in different combinations, was in fact used at Low Ludderburn in earnest. They had no telephone, and Ransome was frequently ill. For everyday convenience, fishing arrangements, and as a safety precaution, they organized a code between Low Ludderburn and Barkbooth, a house right down to the south of the valley. Barkbooth was the home of Colonel Kelsall and his wife, and their two sons Dick and Desmond. The Ransomes were very fond of the two little boys, and frequently took them fishing, cooked feasts for them and told them stories. In return, the boys ran errands until the signals were devised, posed for Ransome's drawings, and offered the youthful company that Ransome seems to have needed to write well.

I had had lunch with Dick and Desmond Kelsall in Oxford early in January. The day before, they had found themselves enjoying the unexpected experience of sailing in a dinghy on the Thames in the suits they had put on for a party to celebrate the publication of Hugh Brogan's *Life of Arthur Ransome* on the centenary of Ransome's birthday. It was held at Ransome's own club, the Garrick, but before the Kelsalls got to it, they were televised reliving the sailing days of fifty years ago.

I looked at Dick hard, but could see no likeness at all to the young, short-sighted, absent-minded professor of *Winter Holiday*. Both Kelsall brothers told me how much fun they had had with the Ransomes, walking up to local tarns or down to the River Winster to fish, travelling in the bone-shaking Trojan, demonstrating the next best thing to a sailing dinghy (their Triang pedal-car converted to a landyacht with a bamboo cane and a tablecloth) and experimenting with home-made bombs made by packing soda-siphon refills with gunpowder.

They were about ten and six when Ransome started *Swallows and Amazons*. After Desmond had read it, Ransome asked him what he thought ought to happen next.

'I said that John was too good. He ought to get over-confident and do something really stupid – like wrecking *Swallow*. Ransome absolutely hooted with laugher, and said that that was exactly what he had planned.'

Dick remembered posing for the photographs, the 'holly-woods', as Ransome used to call them, which helped him with the drawings for *Peter Duck* and *Winter Holiday*.

'And we made the ship's papers for *Swallowdale*. We had a parrot, a grey and red one. We put two pieces of paper round a broomhandle, and covered one of them with a mixture of soot and paraffin. Then we got the parrot to grip first the black one and then the white one with its claws.'

They had enjoyed the signalling between Barkbooth and Low Ludderburn very much; it saved their legs, and made them excellent 'yeomen of signals' on later sailing holidays.

I decided to walk along to Barkbooth to see how the Kelsalls' end of the system had worked. As well as being the Ransomes' contact in emergencies (Square alone = I need help urgently) it was mine. Sheila Caldwell had played tennis with my father-in-law when she was a dashing Arnside belle, and she and her doctor husband had moved into Barkbooth shortly after the Kelsalls left it. All through my stay she let me signal to Oxford on her telephone, and I checked in regularly to reassure the family that I had not drowned in the lake, fallen off a mountain or disappeared into a mineshaft. She also listened to hours of speculations about Ransome, and told me a lot about life in the Lake District today. Now she showed me the barn from which the Kelsalls had signalled to Low Ludderburn.

It was closer to the house than Dick and Dorothea's observatory, and far from ruined. But it was on two floors I went up its steps and inside. On the opposite wall was a winnowing door facing the right way. I worked open its rusty bolts and pulled at it. Sure enough, there was a very good view of what Sheila told me was the end wall of Low Ludderburn – now no longer painted white. Dick had told me that they had used binoculars or a telescope to see the signals because the wall was over a mile away. When I walked round to the outside, at the foot of the barn, Low Ludderburn was hidden by the trees.

The signals themselves were army-style, so it seems likely that they were the brainchild of Colonel Kelsall. The early, simple version in Ransome's handwriting, shown on page 52, is very similar to the signals used in *Winter Holiday*. By February, 1933 the code was of breathtaking complexity. A third signal, a cross, had been added to the basic square and triangle, and all three could be hung at two angles. Dick and Desmond still have their father's copy. The most important single subject was fishing. 'Shall we fish today?' they asked

◇ A   ▢ B   △ C   ▽ D

1. A.   Answer
2. B.   Shall we fish today?
3. C.   Yes
4. D.   No.
5. A.C. I am coming to see you.
6. A.D. Have you any minnows
7. B.C. Weather doubtful.
8. B.D. Will you come to tea?
9. C.A. Shall we fish ~~today~~ Tomorrow?
10. C.B. Flag wag ?!!!! Impossible.
11. D.A. Weather good
12. D.B Weather bad.

each other across the valley. 'Have you any maggots?' 'How many?' For complete security, wrote Ransome in his autobiography, Kelsall always kept his code between padlocked boards. 'There was to be no leakage at his signal station. The fish never had a chance of learning beforehand what was planned for them.' And to his mother he boasted:

There was a great time signalling this morning, between Evgenia and the Kelsalls. The Colonel has added a new signal to our previous two, raising the possible number of signals to 74. He has devised an elaborate code, hoisting one, two or three of the signals in different orders. Evgenia was able to arrange from the terrace of our house yesterday that the Colonel could drive her into Windermere, and that he would call for her for that purpose at three in the afternoon. Great triumph all round.

I walked along the lanes and up the hill to Low Ludderburn, now owned by David and Helen Caldwell. The great yew trees from which the owl hooted as Ransome was writing (so gaining immortality by fooling the sleepy Titty into lighting the Amazons into the secret harbour) are still there; so is the terrace from which the signals were hoisted. The end wall of Low Ludderburn has two windows, one above the other, and once, like the end wall of Holly Howe, it was white-painted. Black signals were hoisted at this end, and white ones against the grey stones of the Kelsalls' barn.

Helen showed me into the old stone barn, the birthplace of the Lake books. 'I have never had, nor ever hope to have, such another workroom as the old barn,' wrote Ransome regretfully, years after he had left the house. It housed a Morris Cowley when the Ransomes first moved in, but it was refloored and given two huge windows with broad cushioned sills. One faces Whitbarrow, a great whale of a fell to the south-east of the hillocky Winster valley, and at it Ransome kept his desk in summer, moving it closer to the new fireplace in winter. On that desk he used to spread the litter of loved objects which he had picked up on his travels – his pocket compass from Reval, a tiny telescope, a sleek green Egyptian cat, a lucky stone from the top of Coniston Old Man: memories made real. There was plenty of room for books, a comfortable chair beside the fire, and acres of floor to pace about on and think. On a shelf a huge pike glared from its glass case (or perhaps it was a perch –

people's memories differ); beside it stood a brass clock and a jar of parrot feathers.

The green parrot was in the family, although it was not Ransome's own. It belonged to his mother, or his sister Joyce, and its feathers were used to make fishing flies rather than pipe cleaners – or Amazon arrows:

> 'Don't bring green parrots for us,' said Nancy. 'Bring them grey with red tails. Then we can feather our arrows with red feathers instead of green ones.'
>
> Captain Flint opened his mouth and shut it again. He looked hard at Nancy Blackett, and then at a jampot on the shelf, in which there was a single green feather and some new pipe-cleaners. Nancy Blackett caught his eye.
>
> 'Your fault for being an enemy,' she said. 'And after all, we didn't take anything but a few feathers. We might have sunk the ship.'

How much gentler was Ransome's own Tittyish concern for the bird, revealed in this letter to his mother:

> Joyce very kindly sent me two parrot feathers. I have put them aside in the hope that when the parrot moults any more I shall have them. You need opposite feathers, you know, to make wings. The colours are excellent, so I hope the parrot will do a good moult and not forget which feathers he has already dropped so that it will be possible to collect the fellows to them. NO HURRY. DO NOT PLUCK THEM.

Most of the contents of Ransome's study can be seen in a little exhibition in the Abbot Hall Museum, a few miles east of Windermere in Kendal. High up a spiral staircase is his desk with all its keepsakes, his favourite pictures and books. At Low Ludderburn the Caldwells had turned up quite a hoard of other mementoes. Helen showed me a much-mended little teapot, made in Russia, a typewriter wheel with Russian characters on it, the bowls of the clay pipes

Ransome loved to smoke and dozens of bottles of stomach powders.

We went into Low Ludderburn itself, ducking our heads. Ransome and Evgenia, who were both tall people, must have banged theirs a good deal until they got used to it. With its deep-silled windows, friendly hearth, and the sun streaming in, it did not look at all the 'savage little place' that Ransome once called it. In his day, though, it had no telephone, electricity or running water. After a welcome cup of coffee, I left, with one last glance at the spectacular view southwards, the contented ducks and chickens, the drifts of daffodils. I took the lane up the hill, and then turned sharply down again to a ford across the River Winster on my way home. In the field near by was a barn almost exactly like Dick's observatory. Ransome must have known it well.

If I was going to find the places in the books as casually as this, completely by luck, my quest was not going to be as straightforward as I had hoped. I began to have a nightmare vision of a jigsaw Swallowdale: a stream here (it was just right), a valley over near Coniston, a cave somewhere else altogether. Still, the lakes had been perfect in atmosphere, if not in every little detail. If I could find places that felt right, like Lanehead, even if they did not exactly fit, I would be happy.

I was still thinking about *Winter Holiday* when I got back to my writing table. There were other sources of inspiration apart from the Kelsalls' signalling. Earliest must have been the great frost of 1895, when Ransome's whole school spent day after day on the ice, lessons cut down to a minimum until Windermere thawed. Like Dick, Arthur saw a perch frozen as if in glass. He saw a coach and four cross the lake, and a whole ox roasted on Bowness Bay. And he saw Herbert Crossley's specially designed Windermere ice yachts, just as Mrs Dixon remembers. 'There were three or four of them rushing about on the lake in '95 and racing for a silver cup,' she tells Dick as he puzzles over sledge-sailing techniques.

There was a faint, breathless cry from Titty, 'A sail! A sail!' and they saw the first of the ice yachts swooping out from between Long Island and the Rio shore.

Dick and Dorothea had never sailed themselves. They could not know what the sight of that white wing gliding past the dark trees meant to the mate of the *Amazon* and the captain and crew of the *Swallow*.

'It's very pretty,' said Dorothea.

She got no answer at all. All five of her new friends were as if stunned. For a minute or two not one of them spoke, and then, as the white sail swept nearer and nearer to the shore, Dorothea heard John say quietly, as if to himself alone, 'Going about, she'll be going about. But how can she?'

Unusually, Arthur Ransome never tells us. So for the benefit of anyone who has ever wondered how ice yachts worked,

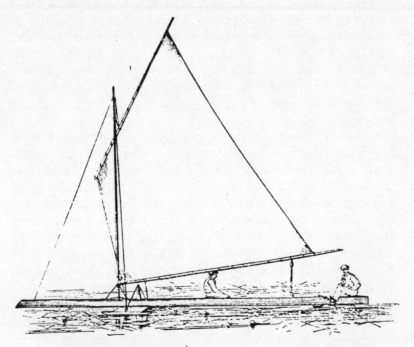

HERBERT CROSSLEY'S WINDERMERE ICE YACHT

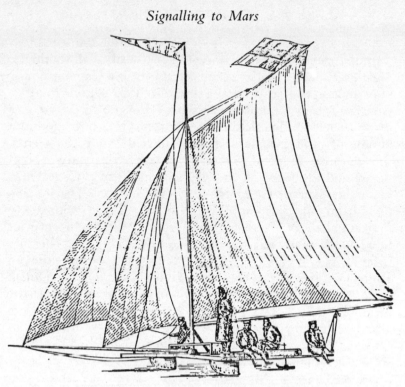

ICE BOAT OF THE SEA OF AZOFF

here is a description of them given by Dixon Kemp in his *Manual of Yacht and Boat Sailing* (a book which Ransome kept on *Racundra*'s bookshelf). They had a spidery wooden framework, thirty-six feet long. Their two side-runners were edged with steel skates, and their two aft runners had glass bullseyes embedded in felt buffers, so that they answered very quickly to the tiller. This was itself tipped with a third skate, which could act as a brake. The rig was lugsail and jib. Ransome also saw the solid and elaborate ice yachts used on the frozen Baltic when he visited the Riga Yacht Club in the winter. But the Windermere yachts were uniquely graceful. Their nearest equivalent today is the Finnish invention of a windsurfer with runners forward and a short directive skeg at the back, which has recently achieved terrifying speeds on ice and packed snow.

There was another great frost in 1929, while Ransome was writing *Swallows and Amazons*. Evgenia walked all round the *Maid Marian*, her diary records, trapped like Captain Flint's houseboat in the ice. And in September 1932 some American fans, the McEoch family, sent what Ransome described as 'a first-rate letter'. The letter does not survive, but I found a bundle of photographs in Leeds labelled 'McEochs'. They show a New England Winter by a lake, with snow everywhere and captions which tell their own story: Cape Horn from the Cape of Good Hope, Buenos Aires, The Persian Gulf from our Landing, Entrance to a Trade Route. My fingers itched to get hold of that letter. Perhaps the germ of Dorothea's character lay in its author. The one clue we have to its contents is in Arthur Ransome's introduction to Pamela Whitlock's and Katharine Hull's book, *The Far-Distant Oxus*,* where he wrote: 'Not content to adopt my stories the McEochs went a stage further and wrote frankly, "We were ashamed of being Swallows and Amazons." Not for them to act over again the adventures of others. They had to invent something new for themselves.' *Winter Holiday* was dedicated to 'The Clan McEoch of Francis Avenue, Cambridge, Massachusetts', which suggests that Ransome owed them something.

Another favourite book of Ransome's was *Bevis*, by Richard Jefferies. Bevis's lake was Coate Water, near Swindon, and his makebelieve was swifter and farther flung than either the McEochs' or Ransome's. He moved from the Mississippi to central Africa, from Romans battling at Pharsalia to New Formosa. The finale of the book is the Antarctic Expedition, but a thaw sets in before Bevis's ice yacht is launched. Instead, the children icebreak through a storm, coming home at dead

---

* *The Far-Distant Oxus* was sent to Ransome by the two schoolgirls who wrote it in 1937. He thought it was so good that he marched into his publisher and announced: 'I have here the best children's book of 1937.' Backed by his introduction and continued support, its authors went on to write two more books about children and ponies on Exmoor, and Pamela Whitlock became one of Ransome's closest and most valued friends.

of night under a sky thick with stars, listening to the great wind blowing from the north. So the story ends:

'We must go to the great sea,' said Bevis. 'Look at Orion!'
The wind went seawards, and the stars are always over the ocean.

Most important of the influences on *Winter Holiday* were the writings of the Norwegian explorer Fridtjof Nansen. Just as the books that the Swallows take to Wild Cat Island (John's *Baltic Pilot*, Part Three, Susan's *Simple Cooking for Small Households*, Titty's *Robinson Crusoe*) set the scene for that story, so the books on the shelf of Captain Flint's houseboat inspire the adventures in *Winter Holiday*.

'Here it is,' said Dick. '*Farthest North*. The Voyage and Exploration of the *Fram* and the Fifteen-Months' Sledge Expedition. This'll tell us everything we want to know.'

Nansen sailed for the North Pole in the specially strengthened *Fram* in 1893, when Ransome was nine, and the story of his adventures was published in 1898. It made him an international hero. He then generously allowed his fellow countryman Amundsen to take *Fram* to the Antarctic, where Nansen's techniques, skis and dog-drawn sledges, proved so much more successful than Captain Scott's ill-fated ponies and motorized sledges.

Ransome met Nansen in 1921 in the Baltic, where Nansen was doing enormously valuable work handling the postwar refugee problem for the League of Nations.

I spent an afternoon sitting with him on the shore of the Gulf of Riga being smilingly scolded for swimming much too far out to sea. He was then and for years afterwards doing more than any other man to mitigate for thousands upon thousands the miseries caused by the political upheavals of those times. I shall always see him as I saw him that day, the great blond Norseman sitting under the tall pines which grow to the very edge of that glittering tide-less sea, the most civilized person of his generation.

The trip to High Greenland which takes place before the try for the Pole was in imitation of Nansen's first expedition, *The First Crossing of Greenland*. Like the Norwegians, Ransome's Polar explorers build an igloo, and then take up residence in a *Fram* of their own. Captain Flint's houseboat is commandeered in his absence for living out the long months in the pack ice, shifting slowly towards the Pole. On his return, he rises nobly to the occasion, even offering the Ds some of his jam. Or he would have, if they hadn't finished it already:

'I'm afraid there isn't any jam,' said Dorothea.
Captain Flint stared at her, got up, and went to the store cupboard.
'Arctic explorers!' he said, looking from one almost empty shelf to another.
'More like locusts, it seems to me.'
'Peggy said it was all meant to be eaten,' said Dorothea.
'So it was,' said Captain Flint. 'And so it has been.'

It is even correct that only Dick and Dorothea make the final dash to the Pole since Nansen made his attempt with only one companion from the *Fram*, Hjelmar Johansen (although Ransome relents enough to allow the rest of the expedition to follow in *his* story).

All the elements in the book were beginning to add up when, on January 3rd, 1933, Ransome noted in his diary that he went to see some neighbours, the Hudsons, and 'heard Colonel Hudson's views on Antarctic and Polar exploration for the *Winter Holiday* book. He wants the children to quarrel!!! and to get stuck in the dark with wet matches. Anyway, he likes the snow idea very much . . . Actually, his ideas don't suggest more than I have already told his children when they were here. But he is a kindly, eager soul.' Colonel Hudson's daughters, Peggy and Joan, had helped by posing for drawings with the

Kelsall boys. One of them had long plaits like Dorothea's, but there the likeness seems to have ended. They were both too young to be in the running as Blacketts.

A few days later, Ransome noted that he 'wrote a letter beginning *Winter Holiday*', and by the end of the month he was conveniently able to skate on Duck Tarn (probably the tiny tarn above Low Ludderburn, which the Caldwells say is always first to be frozen over). A week later he took Taqui, Susan and Titty Altounyan (then at boarding school in Windermere) skating on Tarn Hows. 'Sunshine', he noted. 'Snow on hills, but only on the top. Titty kicking with only one leg, Taqui and Susan getting on pretty fast.'

A little later, John and Susan, skating solemnly by, met Titty almost halfway up the tarn, moving on one foot and kicking herself slowly along with the other. Roger was being pulled along by Dick. Peggy and Dorothea were skating together at the far end, while Captain Nancy, glancing rather nervously over her shoulder, was moving jerkily backwards with a fixed smile on her face.

The Ds prove themselves by skating so well, but Ransome is hard put to make them the centre of the story, and give Peggy a chance, as his notes show him struggling to do. Even with mumps, Captain Nancy runs the whole show. Nothing can keep her down, and the others, for all their efforts, seem puppets in comparison. 'Ought we to go and rope Nancy in?' Peggy, John and Susan ponder as they skate steadily to the rescue of the lost Ds, unaware that at that very moment Nancy has already struggled ahead of them to the Pole. Sitting in front of the fire there with Dick and Dorothea, a mug of hot tea in one hand, and a chicken leg in the other, she says, 'Shiver my timbers! The others will be jolly sick at missing this.' She is not quite crowing, but she is hardly regretful.

IV

Secret Valley

Swallowdale has always haunted me more than any other
Ransome place. I never forgot how 'Titty told of the moor
above the wood, of the waterfall, and of the little valley
above the waterfall, a valley so secret that anybody could
hide in it for ever'.

I was due for another day on Coniston Water, to search for
Swallowdale and to have tea with Brigit Altounyan. I had
spent the previous evening scanning the large-scale Ordnance
Survey map for valleys near the places that Ransome knew
well and I had found three or four possibilities. One was
close to the Walna Scar road, which winds past the foothills
of Kanchenjunga to Duddondale, where Ransome's mother
used to spend holidays. He often walked over from Lanehead
or Low Yewdale to visit her and his sisters. Another was near
the Top o' Selside, behind Nibthwaite. It was the wrong side
of the lake compared with Ransome's map, but there was a
little tarn up there, and it was just the sort of place where
Ransome would have scrambled about as a small boy. A
third was the steep valley above Low Yewdale, where he
used to pitch his tent as a young man. And the fourth was a
little south of the lake itself, up Greenholme Beck. A glance
at the map shows why I could not do the obvious thing, and
follow the stream up from Horseshoe Cove. There is no such
cove on Coniston Water, and just where there should be
trackless moor is the tame, cultivated Torver valley. So I was

going to try and be clever – much too clever, as it eventually turned out.

I drove up to the quarry-road car park, from which people start walking up Coniston Old Man, and took the footpath to the west, the old road to Walna Scar. The countryside did not feel right for Swallowdale to the south, where it ought to have been. There were too many walls and fences and farmsteads. Round to the west, it was wilder, and the map showed waterfalls on the upper reaches of Torver Beck. I set off across a good trackless moor just south of the footpath to find it. Curlews whistled, a buzzard hovered, carrion crows strolled among the sheep. It was desolate enough. But the waterfall turned out to be in an old quarry working, a lethal pit with a spooky lake at the bottom, fed by a waterfall dropping a hundred feet or so down a vertical sheet of rock. I munched mintcake high above it, thankful that Titty and Roger had not come this way in the fog. There was nothing like Swallowdale to be seen, although I walked all the way down Torver Beck, and then circled back to the car park.

The next possibility was Yewdale Beck. Low Yowdale looked strikingly like Dixon's farm. I had found a ground-floor plan of Dixon's which Ransome must have drawn for his own reference when writing the stories, and it seemed just the same as Low Yewdale. I wondered how many steps their staircase had – 'Seven and eight and nine and ten and eleven and that's the dozen,' counted Mrs Dixon on her way up to wake the Callums – but decided that I had no right to disturb its owners. The valley floor there was too flat, and the screes up to the crags too steep to find a Swallowdale – although that part of the fells was a far better bet for old mine workings like Peter Duck's cave than farther south.

I drove down the eastern shore of Coniston Water, re-solutely resisting the almost magnetic attraction of Peel Island, and into Nibthwaite itself. I was going to climb up to the Top o' Selside with the aid of Wainwright's *Guide to the Outlying Fells of Lakeland*. (Every lakeland walker knows Wainwright's witty, informative guides; they are the best possible companions on a climb.) The approach was through the farmgate just behind Swainson's, via an 'unnamed summit' which Ransome called Brockbarrow. I turned right after the gate and took the old track towards Bethecar until I crossed a little stream. Then the guidebook directed me up a murderously steep piece of scree: 'Half an hour's unremitting testing of the trouser buttons during which only two hundred yards' distance will be gained. The track is excessively steep, loose and slippery; gorse offers prickly handholds. At last a fine cairn repays toil.'

I was chanting that final sentence rhythmically to myself by the time I was halfway up, and the reality of gorse as a banister rail was well and truly driven in. At last the superb view of the lake from the cairn did indeed repay toil. I looked almost directly down upon Allan Tarn, a swelling pool in the River Crake just after it flows out of the lake. I had hardly noticed it from ground level, but here I could see it as if drawn on a map – a perfect circle. It was Octopus Lagoon to the life, fringe of reeds and all. It did not matter that it was at completely the wrong end of the lake and flowed out of it rather than into it. There was even a boathouse there that fitted beautifully for the Amazon boathouse. Turning the map on its head like this made it seem even more possible that Swallowdale was up here too. I continued north, very hopefully.

The wild bare tops had all the atmosphere of the High Moor marked near Swallowdale. In the woods below towards the lake, and again eastwards towards Satterthwaite my map marked charcoal-burners' bloomeries and steadings. I could see that a couple of little streams ran down to the lake from here, and one of them, Tarn Beck, looked very promising. Before I reached it, I came across an ancient little quarry. I stopped and looked around. It was a peaceful, sheltered place, with steep rocks at each side, and plenty of room for tents, but there was no stream, and no cave. So I walked on towards Tarn Beck, making detours through untrodden heather to any promising-looking dips, and hoping that the adders were still hibernating. Tarn Beck was a disappointment. It wound flatly over the moor and dribbled

12-13 *Above:* Lanehead (Beckfoot) as it looks today. Close by is Bank Ground Farm (*below*), model for Holly Howe and holiday home for Taqui, Susan, Titty, Roger and Brigit.

14-15 The Amazon boathouse is at the south end of Coniston Water. Inside there is still a native war canoe and *Mavis* (*right*), the original *Amazon*.

16-18 *Above:* some features of Peel Island in Coniston Water inspired Wild Cat Island. Taqui Altounyan sits at Titty's lookout. *Below right:* the secret harbour. *Below left:* Roger Altounyan, watching out for wild boar in Syria, could have posed for the frontispiece of *Pigeon Post.*

19-20 Expedition to Swallowdale. The author's children scale Watch Tower Rock (*above*) to look at Kanchenjunga. *Below:* another part of Swallowdale, the Knickerbockerbreaker, is far away on the other side of the lake, behind Swainson's Farm in Nibthwaite.

down the slope to the lake, without a single waterfall of any size. I followed it upstream to Arnsbarrow Tarn, a lovely lonely place, edged with peat hags and rushes. Could Roger have clutched his trout here?

From the tarn it was only a short climb to the Top o' Selside (1,091 ft). From its summit, the lake was completely hidden, but fells spread endlessly away to the snowy tops of Helvellyn to the north and Wetherlam and the Old Man to the west. Next came the easy bit. After a short scramble, a cart track takes walkers back down to Nibthwaite, winding high above the lake and giving very good views all the way. Swinging happily downhill, with lunch in mind, I suddenly had to come to a stop. A stream ran under the track through a little stone bridge, although not an arched one, and a tight fit to scramble under. Waterfalls. Below the track the stream ran down through woods to the lake. There was no help for it. I would have to climb uphill again beside the Selside Beck, as the map named it, to what could conceivably be Swallow-dale, just over the horizon. I thought of the laden Captain Flint with respect, hummed 'Wayhay and up she rises', admired the potential swimming pools and graceful birch trees. Disappointingly, the top revealed no secret valley, just a boggy, tussocky petering-out of the stream up on the moor. It *was* very close to the old quarry. Would some heavy rainfall make a difference? I ate my picnic lunch there; then, unsatisfied, went on down the hill, noting the great sheets of rock tilted into the ground. Next week I would get my family to decide which of them was the Knickerbocker-breaker of Ransome's childhood. Another reason for think-ing that Swallowdale must be somewhere here had been that, in the book, Roger's Knickerbockerbreaker is one side of the secret valley's walls.

It was still too early to visit Brigit Altounyan. I was heartily sick of hunting for Swallowdale, and the sun and wind looked just right for a different sort of exploration. I drove along to Rigg Wood beach, with its brand-new wooden jetty waiting for the newly restored *Gondola*'s first voyage of the season. There was Peel Island again. The only problem was that I had no spare clothes. If I fell in, I would have to arrive at Brigit's house extremely damp. The Bridget in *Secret Water* wouldn't mind that, I was sure, especially after her narrow escape from the Red Sea.

I rigged up the board, watched curiously by some woodmen with chainsaws, modern descendants of charcoal-burners. The lake was completely empty, except for a fishing boat just to the west of the island. Perhaps the perch are still bigger there, just as Taqui remembered.

Once away from the shelter of the headland, I found out two things very quickly. Firstly, I was sailing much faster than I had intended; secondly, my two practice sessions had been useful. Hardly wobbling at all, I even (briefly) adopted a stylish side-tilted stance, driving the board forwards with my front foot like the experts. Peel Island looked even better close to, its long mossy flanks plunging into the water, plenty of trees on top, and to the south the straggling rocks of the secret harbour. I tacked to and fro until I was lined up with the beach, and then came straight in as Captain Nancy directed, waggling the sail backwards and forwards to keep some way. Gently, the board grounded on the fine shingle of the little beach, and I stepped off – an Amazon, home at last.

It didn't take long to explore the island. It is only about half the size of Blakeholme, a little paradise of winding paths, mossy rocks, and shady trees. There is no room for the decent-sized camp that a housewife like Susan demanded, although I could see the dip between two ramparts of rock where W.G. Collingwood said he had found the traces of Viking life which inspired his adventure story, *Thorstein of the Mere*. Equally there was barely room for Titty to have avoided the Amazons, let alone enough space for the massive charge launched against Captain Flint at the end of *Swallow-dale*. Like Blakeholme, Peel Island could do with being towed out to sea a little farther. It would not be difficult to swim to it.

I think that on balance, given Ransome's own evidence, Blakeholme has to remain as Wild Cat Island, improved with

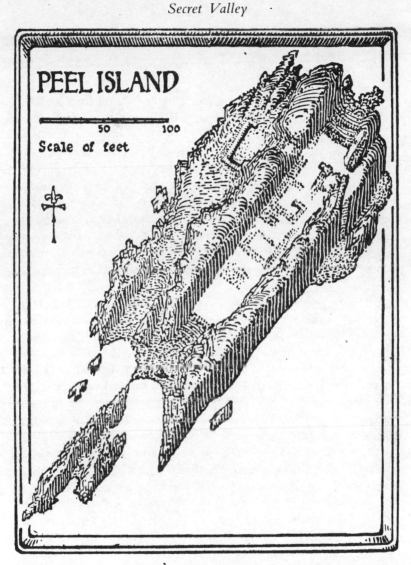

W.G. COLLINGWOOD'S MAP OF HIS EXCAVATIONS ON
PEEL ISLAND

Peel Island's harbour. But Peel Island has another claim to a
place in Ransome's world. As the rough draft of *Peter Duck*,
'Their Own Story', makes clear (see page 148) the little green

schooner, the *Wild Cat*, was named after an island which looked just like a ship. That was not Blakeholme but Peel Island, and the idea came from *Thorstein of the Mere*:

In the midst of Thurstonwater [the old name for Coniston Water] is a little island, lying all alone. When you see it from the fells, it looks like a ship at anchor, while all the mere moves upbanks or downbanks as the wind may be. The little island is shiplike also because its shape is long and its sides are steep, with no flat or shelving shores, but a high short nab there is to the northward, for a prow, so to speak; and a high sharp ness to the southward for poop. And to make the likeness better still, a long narrow calf rock lies in the water, as if it were the cockboat at the stern, while the tall trees stand for masts and sails.

Perhaps another incident in that book, when Thorstein saves his tomboy friend Raineach from a wild cat, put the idea for the island's name into Ransome's mind. Even if it was not quite Wild Cat Island, Peel Island was, as Susie Altounyan had said in her letter, a gem of a place, and I shared her hope that it would never be overrun or spoilt. At that moment there was no litter, no names carved, no swarms of craft making for it from every corner of the lake. Long may it stay that way.

I waggled out of the harbour again and had the best sail of the trip, circumnavigating the little green ship, admiring it from every angle, and eventually taking long tacks back to Rigg Wood. Miraculously dry, I drove back to Nibthwaite, where Brigit Altounyan now lives. She is married, and has children with children of their own, who play on the shores of the lake just as their great-grandparents and Arthur Ransome did. Brigit is researching into the history of the Collingwood side of her family, so she was very ready to be both interested and helpful when I explained the problems and excitements I had found while delving into Captain Flint's trunk.

'I was only a baby, much younger than the others when

they first met Arthur Ransome,' she told me. 'The time that I really got to know him was when he visited us in Syria, when he was writing *Peter Duck* up at the top of the house. He brought us a sailing dinghy called *Peter Duck*, so we had two boats on the lake there, instead of just the leaky old *Beetle II*.'

I asked her about his characterization of her brothers and sisters.

'It was certainly true that we were independent – unusually so. My father used to take us off for long treks in the Amanus mountains above the village of So'oukolouk, and we camped in tree houses, and ate roasted wild boar round camp fires.'

She showed me an old photograph of Roger on one of those treks, sitting on the branch of a tree with snake-boots laced high up his shins, every inch the ship's boy of the *Wild Cat*.

'Camping always had to be done properly, whether we were in Syria or in England. No paper was allowed when lighting fires; even today Roger won't hear of using camping gas or anything like that. We used to have army-type sleeping bags in canvas rolls, carried on donkeys. Or at home we used a sail as a tent, and weighed down its sides with stones.'

I asked Brigit about a letter which had been puzzling me. It had been sent by her grandfather, W.G. Collingwood, to Arthur Ransome, just after he had read *Swallows and Amazons* for the first time. After saying how much he liked the book, Collingwood wrote:

Somehow you have made your Titty so very like my Titty, and in a degree your Ruth-Nancy is more like my Ruth than can be expected unless you had seen her last month being a savage with a woodland lair which was quite realistic. Unfortunately, she has no Titty to join her pranks and they fizzle out for want of support, but she is a true pirate at heart.

Who was this Ruth? Could she be the key to Nancy the

ruthless? Brigit looked at the family tree she had drawn up.

'It might have been my uncle Robin's daughter Ruth. She was born in 1921. She would have been about ten then. She had a brother, William, who was two years older. But they lived in Oxford. Maybe she had come up for a holiday with the grandparents.'

That sounded a little young for Nancy. Yet Ruth Collingwood was clearly a playmate of Titty's, and the name might well have come from her, as a compliment to his friend Robin, who had taught him to sail.

Brigit told me that another childhood acquaintance, Pauline Rawdon-Smith, now Pauline Marshall, had called on her a couple of years ago. She and her older sister Georgina and their brother Rawdon had often visited their parents' cousin, Miss Holt, at Tent Lodge, a house very close to Lanehead, and they had met the Altounyans when they were at Bank Ground Farm. Pauline Marshall had also sent me some interesting letters about her childhood beside the lake. There seemed a real possibility that the sight of the two little girls – a tomboyish pair, to judge from early photographs of them – could have put Ransome in mind of his Amazon pirates. They used to wear shorts, which was unusual for girls at that time; even the Altounyan girls tucked their skirts into their knickers. Pauline remembers playing at semaphore, quacking like a duck, and parachuting from trees into the lake holding on to an umbrella. She also remembers being introduced to Ransome himself one day, and although that was the only time she did meet him, feels that he might have taken in their characters very quickly. Certainly, the only clues which Ransome gives to the Blacketts was that one day he saw two girls in red caps playing by the side of the lake. Pauline became a sailing instructor, the right sort of fate for Peggy; and she is the inventor of an ingenious seat called the Able Sailor, which makes it possible for handicapped sailors to change sides while tacking.

It may be an obstinate streak in me, but I was not convinced that the astonishingly vivid character of Nancy sprang fully fledged from so casual an acquaintance. I told

Brigit about my suspicion that her mother Dora and her aunt Barbara might have inspired the invention of Peggy and Nancy. As teenagers they had taught Arthur Ransome to sail in the original *Swallow*. Moreover, in Ransome's original notes for the book, the Blackett girls had had a brother much younger than they were, just like Robin Collingwood. I had read letters which Barbara had written to Ransome while he was in Russia: clearly she was an extremely strong personality, with a passion for Joseph Conrad, one of the greatest of all tellers of tales about the high seas. Brigit showed me a picture of Dora and Barbara in their early twenties, and for all the old-fashioned costume I felt that there was something of Nancy and Peggy about them, something which Dora's daughter Taqui seemed to have inherited. Such a mixture of generations was in keeping with the way Ransome wove his childhood experiences in with the present in his stories.

Brigit and her husband John showed me round Nibthwaite. I had half-expected the bridge which Ransome mentions climbing under as a boy to have been the round-arched one of the picture in *Swallowdale*, but it was smaller and flatter, carrying the road over Caws Beck. We went down to take a closer look at Allan Tarn. John explained that it was typical of a tarn associated with glacial moraines formed thousands of years ago. We wandered among the alders and reeds and imagined the waterlily octopi of summer. Brigit began to plan a canoe in which they could paddle down the river. The Swallows' adventures might not be altogether over, I decided. This seemed to be just how Brigit should have grown up, to be a web-footed grandmother teaching her grandchildren to enjoy the lake.

One of the grandchildren came up, another Robin, only three but tall for his age. His father Chris suggested a look at the boathouse, the one at the mouth of the river which had looked so right for the Amazon boathouse from Brockbarrow. Inside was a native war canoe, old-style with curly iron seats. There was also a white-painted, fourteen foot sailing dinghy with a patched brown lugsail: *Mavis*, still here after fifty-five years. Five minutes later I was satisfying the ambition of a lifetime: rowing the original *Amazon* on to the lake and towards the Octopus Lagoon. In the bows sat Robin, fifth-generation ship's boy. It wasn't quite perfect. I would have preferred to be sailing her, but Chris was about to leave for London, and she had to be put away very soon.

Then Brigit took me to see Swainson's itself, the farmhouse where Ransome had stayed as a boy. It doesn't look like the drawings in *Swallowdale*, although some near-by farm cottages and barns do. It is a more upright, formal house where Swainsons lived without a break for over a hundred years. Round at the back it was more recognizable. There was the stone-paved passage along which Mary Swainson had clattered to meet Roger and Titty, to ask them to help her churn butter just as she had asked the boy Arthur. There is still a huge old-fashioned range in the back-kitchen, and I could imagine ninety-year-old grandfather Swainson singing hunting songs beside it while his wife patiently quilted. There are damsons in the orchard, holes for beehives in the thick stone walls, and an odd little shed which Ransome mentions in his *Autobiography*: 'I had to glance into the earth closet in the garden, with its three sociable seats, two for grown-ups and one small one for a baby in the middle, to see that there had been no change in the decoration of its walls. These were papered with pages from *Punch*.' Peering in apprehensively, I can report the disappearance of the pages from *Punch*, and also, oddly, of the small central seat. The rest remains a convenient place for potting geraniums.

I asked Brigit and John about the elusive Swallowdale.

'Caves sound like Wetherlam,' said John, pointing on the map to the mountain on the eastern side of the Old Man range. 'It's riddled with old mine-workings; they call them the hundred holes of Wetherlam. Or there's Beacon Tarn across the Crake, over there.'

I looked at Beacon Tarn, and Beacon Hill beside it. A stream from the Crake, the Greenholme Beck, wound up to the south of it. Beacon Hill had been one of the possibilities I had found the night before. It had the added merit for the literalist that it was extremely close to where Swallowdale was drawn on Ransome's own map. There was just time to explore it that afternoon, refuelled by the enormous tea I had enjoyed.

I crossed the River Crake at Water Yeat, and took a little track up to Greenholme farm, an idyllic place. A donkey peered over a wall, two ponies played together in the field, some ducks waddled up to inspect my car. The farmer appeared, brandishing a baby's bottle full of milk. 'Want some?' he shouted cheerfully, and disappeared into his barn to feed the lambs. I parked the car, and walked up a grassy track to another Tarn Beck, this time a tributary of the Greenholme Beck. It wasn't quite right. Titty and Roger had come up from the lakeside, not the river, but there had been a bridge under the road, and here were some lovely larch woods. The beck was doing all it should – leaping down little waterfalls, and then flattening out as I reached the moor above.

I looked around. Swallowdale? There were steep rocky sides to the little valley there, and a good place for tents, although in summer thick heather might make it more difficult. There was another little waterfall ahead, just where it should be. The farmtrack was a pity. This was hardly a secret valley, and there was no cave, for all that the heather was hanging in promising clumps over the rocks.

I decided to give Selside Beck four out of ten, and this valley six out of ten. Peter Duck's cave was a problem. If it was an old mine working, it was unlikely to be at this end of the lake. Perhaps Ransome had had to cheat, had found the Swallows desperately outmanoeuvred as the Amazons dashed through the bracken towards them, and had grabbed it off Wetherlam to help them. Could that have been why it had to be Peter Duck's cave? Because it was as much a fantasy as Peter Duck himself?

Bother Swallowdale, I thought. It was taking up far too much of my time. 'Trout Tarn,' we are told, 'was nearly a mile beyond Swallowdale, high on the top of the moor.' Beacon Tarn fitted that all right, and it is such a beautiful

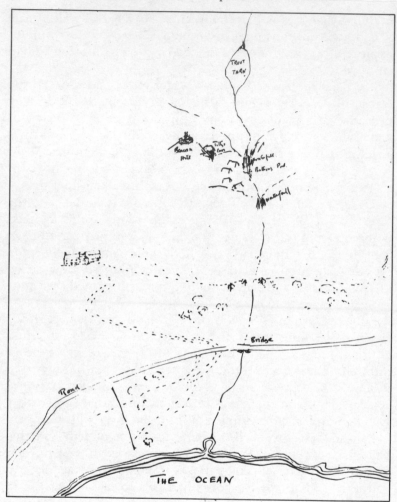

ARTHUR RANSOME'S UNPUBLISHED WORKING SKETCH
FOR SWALLOWDALE

place that even for explorers totally uninterested in Swallowdale it is worth a visit. It has a little beach for Roger to guddle
his trout on, a path all round it, and a real watch tower near
by, Beacon Hill, a signal point that once warned of Viking
raiders and was manned again in the Second World War.

From its summit cairn I looked round at the sharp grey outcrops of rocks, the streams hurrying away in all directions, and realized that Swallowdale could equally well be on this northern side. There were plenty of rocks high enough to keep watch from – too many, really.

Head spinning and feet aching, I got back to the car and drove home along the southern road to Newby Bridge, then along the east side of Windermere until I came to a turning marked Great Tower Scout Camp. This lane cuts past the Ludderburns to the Winster valley. At the top is Moor How.

I stopped the car by a stream that tumbled down some little waterfalls and with weary recognition studied the sloping rocks rearing out of the fields. They looked suspiciously like those in Clifford Webb's drawings of Swallowdale. The map revealed that the stream trickled down behind Low Ludderburn to the River Winster. Almost too convenient. I refused to believe that this was Swallowdale, but one thing was becoming evident – Ransome country was everywhere around me. It was a state of mind rather than a place.

I haven't included all the other ambitious forays I made in search of Swallowdale, round Bigland, Cartmel, Rusland, and Satterthwaite, because one rainy day, when sifting through Ransome's working notebooks, which are kept at Abbot Hall, I came upon the cast-iron evidence I needed. It was a sketchmap of Swallowdale, a very early one, in which the cave is called Titty's Cave instead of Peter Duck's. On it the Watch Tower, which was to end up to the north of the camp, was set squarely south of it. With a name. Beacon Hill. Proof positive. When the children arrived, we would make an expedition up the stream which I could see winding down from Beacon Hill across Stable Harvey Moss. I would lead them straight to Swallowdale, set deep into the northern side of the beacon. Almost exactly, in fact, where it should have been all along. I had been too clever by half.

V

Kanchenjunga Beckons

Swallowdale, the longest of the Ransome books, is about much more than a secret valley. In it, the lake country comes to life: the boat-builders of Bowness, the woodmen, the charcoal-burners, the Grasmere sports, and, most vivid of all perhaps, the hound trails. I realized that these were still very much part of Cumbrian life, as I listened to the local radio discussing form and advising punters on which dog might be a good bet. Melody, the leader of the hounds that ran through Swallowdale, took her name from one of Ransome's favourite Cartmel pubs, the 'Hark to Melody' with its signboard painting of a pack of hounds in full cry. Today the best place to watch a trail is probably at Langdale, where most of the course is in view.

Arthur Ransome's first draft of *Swallowdale* was about a straightforward war between the 'tribe' of the Swallows with their sacred totem Bustillian and 'Caliban Flint' and the Amazon pirates. Exploration rather than shipwreck led them to a new camp much later on in the story, and the climax was the theft of the totem and 'Titty in pursuit'. There was mention of a cairn and a beacon fire. What happened? My guess is that Nancy was hogging too much of the limelight as usual. Ransome's defence was to shackle the Blacketts to Great-aunt Maria, so that the Swallows could enjoy a little undisturbed housekeeping, fishing and boat-repairing.

Swallowdale was also a chance to use more of Ransome's own memories. In 1909, when he had had very little more sailing experience than Captain John, he came close to shipwreck in *Jamrach*, the Tent Lodge half-decker:

> With a light southerly wind and sunshine, I tacked down the lake, thinking I should have an easy run back. I was about a quarter of a mile from Peel Island when the wind fell away altogether. Suddenly I heard a shrill hissing and looked over my shoulder to see a black sky, a black lake, and a sharp line of white from shore to shore. I had no steerage way, and could not turn to meet what was coming. Nor had I time. One moment I was drifting in a dead calm. The next the squall was upon us, and before the boat could ease things by moving, the boom had flicked upright and over, there had been a violent jibe, the jaws of the gaff had smashed, the mast and sail had slapped into the water, and poor old *Jammy* was lying on her beam ends. I hauled down the sail by main force, and she righted, when I found myself sitting in the water, with the lake splashing round and over the coamings of the well. The violence of the squall had passed, but it was now blowing strongly from the north, driving the wreck towards the rocks at the northern end of the island.

He was saved by his bootlaces, stout leather ones, with which he made a makeshift support for the gaff and just managed to get enough wind into the remains of the sail to clear the rocks. It was 'black night' before he got back to the head of the lake under jury rig, reproaching himself for being a careless fool much as the skipper of *Swallow* did.

One of the highlights of the later part of the book is the conquest of Kanchenjunga. The Old Man (2,631 ft), according to Wainwright's *Southern Fells*, 'bears the same relation to Coniston village as the Matterhorn to Zermatt'; the Matterhorn was the old Blackett name for it, and they, like the Ransomes and the Collingwoods, had a family tradition of getting to the top of it as young as possible. Ransome boasted that, carried up by his father as a baby, he was 'the youngest ever to have been at the summit'. So the little box which

Roger found tucked inside the cairn, with its Victorian farthing and proud claim that Jim Turner, Molly Blackett and Bob Blackett 'climbed the Matterhorn' in 1901, was a way of emphasizing that the stories mix together the experiences of at least three generations of Coniston families. It also cast an unusually sombre shadow.

'That's mother and Uncle Jim,' said Peggy in a queer voice.
'Who is Bob Blackett?' asked Susan.
'He was father,' said Nancy.

Ransome's own father had died when he was thirteen, as a result of an injury to his foot while fishing several years before. His death marked the end of their holidays at Nibthwaite.

Brilliant early morning sunshine, a light frost, and a flat calm marked the right day to get up early and climb the Old Man myself. I took the ferry across the middle of Lake Windermere; it moved like a painted ship upon a painted ocean, past moored boats twinned by immaculate reflections. There was the Hen Rock and her attendant Chicken, Belle Isle and its pepperpot mansion, the Lilies and sturdy Rampholme. Coniston had barely opened its eyes, and mine was the second car (nearly a record) in the quarry car park at the foot of the mountain. To do the thing properly, of course, I should have made a halfway camp last night, but at least I was climbing Kanchenjunga as early as the explorers did.

Starting along the path map in hand, I found it very different from Ransome's description. There was only one small wood for the children to climb up through, just north of Copper Mines Beck, and it was hard to ignore the whole of Coniston village unless I pretended that it had sunk into the bottom of the Octopus lagoon. It is clearly stated that the expedition scaled the northern side of Kanchenjunga, so it was no good wondering if they had come up Torver Beck, a much better wooded stream, despite the bottomless pit of the old quarry. Still, I found a good place beside some mossy rocks where they might have spent the night, imagined them there for a while, and then went on.

With no companions to help me up (or down) with a rope, I took the usual route, the quarry road. There are some spectacular distractions that Nancy and her companions were too busy climbing to mention: the gaping mouth of the main quarry with deep chasms at its sides, the stunning petrol blue of Low Water, with Brim Fell sweeping round above it. That was where Roger saw the goats ('the word ended with a squeak'), but there are only sheep around today. Then I had to tackle the nasty work of picking a way through the sharp-edged rubble of loose stones which carpets this approach. The thousands of walkers who climb the Old Man every year are wearing this part of it away. At last the stones thinned out into springy grass and snowdrifts, and I saw the cairn at the very top. The explorers each reacted to the sight of it in typically different ways; characterized in a nutshell:

With the cairn that marked the summit now in full view before them, they wriggled out of the loops in the rope and raced for it. John and Nancy reached the cairn almost together. Roger and Titty came next. Mate Susan had stopped to coil the rope and Mate Peggy had waited to help her carry it.

Another early bird arrived, in very correct mountain dress: thick boots and socks, bare shins and breeches, and a colossal knapsack hung about with useful equipment. It had a duvet in it, he explained, in case it got so cold that he had to bivouac on the peak. We both looked down at the hills and valleys below, and while he clicked away with his camera he let me use his field glasses to scan the old mine workings. He was a geologist, camping out on near-by Goat's Water and vetting the place for a team which was going to do a survey later in the year. I asked him about copper, and he told me what pyrites looked like, and a little about the cubic structure of quartz. The instant friendship which develops between any two people on a mountain top began to dissolve as we saw an ant-like procession of other climbers winding its way up far below. Rush-hour had started. Time to move on.

I walked along the snowy ridge between the Old Man and Brim Fell to take in the view. The Isle of Man's mountains were shadowy on the western horizon, and what I hoped were Scotland's Galloway Hills could have been cloudbanks. There was no sign of Wales or Ireland, the other two of the five kingdoms supposedly visible from the top of the Old Man, but the lakeland peaks were startlingly clear: Scafell, Skiddaw, Helvellyn, Ill Bell, and High Street, just as Nancy catalogued them.

The cairn was almost crowded on the way back, so I decided to take the southern route down, one which Wainwright says is infinitely better than the quarry road M1. It gave me a very good view of Beacon Hill, and I thought of John raising his telescope to look at Watch Tower Rock. 'There was the rock, and the dark patch of water in the middle of the heather that they knew was Trout Tarn. Just beyond the rock must be Swallowdale itself.' I hoped so.

Next day I left the lakes and went a hundred miles south to meet Squashy Hat's daughter. *Pigeon Post* is dedicated to Oscar Gnosspelius, who had spent several years as a surveyor in South Africa and South America. In the Transvaal he met prospectors, and when he returned to the Lake District he took up hunting for precious metals himself. Thanks to him, wrote Ransome,

> I believe there are no mining errors in the book . . . He gallantly threw himself into the business of my prospecting children, lecturing me on gosson, veins, reefs, pyrites and what not, demonstrating with the tools he had himself used the methods of panning and washing, and taking me up Wetherlam to make sure of the details of Slater Bob's activities and the ancient tunnels on the hill.

Among the tools that 'he had himself used' were a large mortar and pestle with a piece of leather wrapped round its handle. In Chapter XXII of *Pigeon Post* there is a picture of

Nancy, in goggles, crushing the promising quartz from the
S.A.D.M.C.'s gulch. Janet, Oscar's daughter, posed for the
drawing, and she still has that pestle and mortar. In a letter
she had told me that as well as being provider of technical
information for *Pigeon Post*, her father 'was then taken as the
model for the (overdrawn) Squashy Hat; but not in his own
hat'. I was sorry that the hat was wrong, but I knew Janet
was right. At the end of a letter to his mother just after the
book came out, Ransome had added a postscript: 'You are
quite right about Squashy Hat and Gnossie.'

Janet, an architect by profession, with a deep interest in
local history, turned out to be well-informed on Ransome
country. Her family lived at Lanehead with her grandfather,
W.G. Collingwood, until 1933, and then moved to High
Hollin Bank, still close by Coniston Water, until 1965. On
July 5th, 1929, Ransome went to tea with them at Lanehead,
and noted in his diary the news he heard: 'Oscar Gnosspelius
has found copper on Old Man.' Janet explained that he
would have been referring to the prospecting level on
Brimfell above the old Dixon's works, started early in 1929
by her father and John William Shaw. The Shaws are a
lakeland mining family of very long standing, and John
William Shaw was undoubtedly pictured as Slater Bob.
Four or five years later, when the yield of Brimfell mine proved

81

disappointingly tiny, Oscar Gnosspelius set Shaw up in the
Penny Rigg Quarry, at the foot of near-by Wetherlam, to
make a living from quarrying the fine green slate there. The
layout of Penny Rigg is exactly that of the old quarry
through which Nancy leads the prospectors in search of Slater
Bob. There is a long tunnel and then 'a lofty chamber in the
rock'. Janet remembered her father taking Ransome there in
June 1935 to visit Shaw and to explore the Tilberthwaite
Copper Mine higher up Wetherlam. The copper mines were
once linked to Penny Rigg quarry by the Tilberthwaite Deep
Level, a tunnel over 3,000 feet long driven through the hillside
to bring the copper out of the mines, the tunnel rashly used by
the hurrying moles:

The small procession hurried on. For a long time there was
no talking.
'It must go right through the hill,' said Dorothea at last.
'It'll come out on the other side where the quarries are,'
said Roger.
'But that's miles and miles,' said Titty. 'And we've got
to get back.'
'Will the torches last?' said Roger. Their second torch
was already growing dim.
'There's still mine,' said Dorothea.
'I say,' said Titty. 'Perhaps this is the Old Level. Nancy
did say that it's supposed to go right through. Perhaps
Squashy Hat was talking to Slater Bob and came back this
way.'

Janet spread out a six-inch-to-the-mile geologists' map of
Wetherlam and the Old Man. The notes on it, she told me,
were partly her father's and partly those of her grandfather,
W.G. Collingwood. So this was the very map Squashy Hat
sat looking at, unaware that he was being watched.
(' "Giminy. He's in the middle of prospecting," Nancy
almost shouted.') I could see the twists of the rocky contours,
and marks suggesting faults and possible lodes. High Topps,
then, was not on the south-eastern slopes of the Old Man,

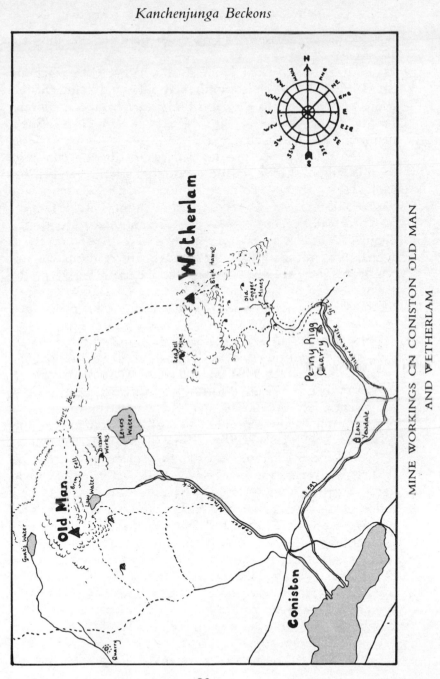

MINE WORKINGS ON CONISTON OLD MAN
AND WETHERLAM

but on the south-eastern slopes of Wetherlam, the 'hill of a 100 holes'.

On impulse, I asked Janet if she had any ideas about Strickland Junction, the station where Titty and Roger change trains on their way to Rio, and find a carrier pigeon waiting for Mr Roger Walker (' "It's Nancy," cried Titty. "She's beginning something already." ')

'Is there a picture of it?' Janet explained how accurate in local details she had found Ransome's illustrations to be. We looked at it together. To me it showed a fairly average steam engine and three very average Ransome figures beside it.

'That wall, behind the engine. Oxenholme. No doubt about it. There is a very long high wall at the station there which blots out the view over Kendal.' We read on, and she confirmed that the 'farmhouse not unlike Holly Howe' could still be seen from the train, and that there would be a glimpse of the lake from the windows before the train drew into Windermere station.

Over lunch, Janet helped me with many other small details, and contributed ideas of her own. In February 1963, when Windermere had frozen over, she had been walking on Bowness Bay. At the point jutting out just north of it, behind the Yacht Club, she had seen an old wooden summerhouse which immediately reminded her of the drawing of the North Pole in *Winter Holiday*. It must have been known to Ransome and his schoolfriends as they played about on the frozen bay; perhaps it even played that part in one of their games. It is no longer there today, unfortunately, but I had found no sign of anywhere else that would do for the Pole, except for Storr's Temple and that was much too far south.

Janet pointed out that the personalities of Ransome's own brother and sisters might have contributed to the characters of the Swallows. She said that Joyce, like Titty, was imaginative and eventually wrote children's books. Geoffrey, 'a Roger-type', was mechanically minded, and was a printer in Edinburgh until he was killed in the First World War. Cecily became a schoolmistress.

I asked her whether there were any charcoal-burners still

about in lakeland. I knew Ransome had many friends among them, and had brought burns, professional or amateur, into three of the five lake books, *Swallows and Amazons, Swallowdale* and *Pigeon Post.*

'His house at The Heald is a good place to start looking for past signs of them,' she told me. 'If you walk up into the woods, you'll find quite a lot of flat, round patches set into the steep hillside. They are old pitsteads. Scratch the ground and you'll find charcoal. In fact,' and she turned to her desk, 'have this: it's just up your street.' She handed me a leaflet by the Woodmanship Trust. It announced a two-day event at Brantwood, Ruskin's house, close by The Heald, in September, which included a 'traditional charcoal burn'. I found out later that there is still a very old 'Billy' living at Spark Bridge, who has passed on the ancient secrets of his trade to preserve them. So the savages should live on.

They rowed away down the lake. The dark came fast overhead. Stars shone out. Owls were calling. The edges of the lake disappeared under the hills. They could see the outlines of the hills, great black masses, pressing into the starry sky . . .
Suddenly high in the darkness they saw a flicker of bright flame. There was another and then another, and then a pale blaze lighting a cloud of smoke. They all looked up towards it as if they were looking at a little window, high up in a black wall. As they watched, the figure of a man jumped into the middle of the smoke, a black, active figure, beating at the flames. The flames died down, and it was as if a dark blind were drawn over the little window. Then a new flame leapt up and again the man was there, and then that flame died like the others and there was nothing but the dark.
'It's savages,' said Titty. 'I was sure there must be some somewhere in those woods.'

On the next sunny day I went to look at Wetherlam, a broad, sprawling hill just north of Coniston village, and at 2,502 ft only a little lower than its neighbour, the Old Man. A narrow road turns off the main A593 and winds along to Tilberthwaite Gill. There is a car park just after the ruined Penny Rigg Quarry, and a good footpath up the north side of the stream. I took with me Eric Holland's very detailed guide, *Coniston Copper Mines*, and a torch, although I was not planning to grope down any of the old mine workings. They are very dangerous indeed. Venturing into the Old Level was probably the most idiotic thing which any of Ransome's characters ever did, as he tried to make clear by Slater Bob's horror at the sight of the children coming out of the tunnel, and by the horrid scene of the disappearing string.

> Just then John came back out of the tunnel. He had a cut end of string in his hand and was coiling it up. He unfastened the other end of the string from the clump of heather. His face had gone quite white, and he looked queerly at Titty and Roger.

The walk up beside the deep rocky cleft through which Tilberthwaite Beck plunges down the hillside is a spectacular one, and the dark mouths of the old tunnels can even be seen behind the waterfalls. As the hillside flattened out, I saw the old workings of the copper mines. They never repaid the many thousands of pounds sunk into them and have been deserted for more than half a century. I was surprised that they were not well fenced off. Only a few scraps of wire hung round even the worst of the chasms, slimy green vertical drops from which even a mountain goat would be hard put to escape. Still, it was fine country for High Topps, particularly the long sweep of fell southwards to Yewdale Crag. The cliff-like sides of Wetherlam looked right for Ransome's Grey Screes, and though the next valley north was called Greenburn instead of Greenbanks, it did sport an Atkinson's Coppice. Squashy Hat stayed at Atkinson's farm.

To take a view of the scene, I climbed up the eastern shoulder of Wetherlam to Birk Fell. It was a good enough lookout, but I decided to do the thing properly and climb

Wetherlam itself. It was much less of a beaten track than the path up Kanchenjunga. I hadn't seen a soul all afternoon, except for some pussyfeet picnicking down in the valley, and I was fantasizing in fine Dorothea-style about the mountain rescue team hunting for my corpse in a mineshaft while I was buried in a snowdrift up here when a rock in front of me stirred.

'Is this the top?' I asked.

'Yes. Well done,' it replied, unwinding several layers of scarves from its head and offering me a protein-packed health-food biscuit to celebrate.

We exchanged views on views companionably, and then went our separate ways. From the top of Wetherlam I could see the pattern of the old workings lower down, travelling systematically across the fell towards the southern flanks of the hill, Lower Hows.

'But what's it for?' said Nancy.

They were looking at a great patch of white paint on the face of a rock a long way up the steep slopes of Grey Screes. There seemed no reason for it at all . . .

They climbed, sometimes on hands and knees on the rocks, sometimes skirting round a bit of crag too steep to climb. They came, breathless, to the second of the white patches. Standing beside it they could see another higher still . . .

'I wonder if it's the same crack going all the way up the hill,' said Dick . . .

He was very near the truth, but threw away the idea in favour of Nancy's theory: 'Galoots we are. Gummocks. Mutton-headed gummocks. He's only pretending . . . He's guessed that Slater Bob's told us something he hasn't told him. He comes up here just to have an excuse for watching us.'

Holland's *Coniston Copper Mines* helped me to trace the North Lode, as this vein of copper was called, as it crosses Lower Hows. Then, he writes, 'it strikes towards the God's Blessing vein'. W.T. Shaw's *Mines in the Lake District* had more to say about God's Blessing, the name of one of the most ancient of the workings in the neighbouring Copper Mines Valley. It is almost four hundred years old and was reputed to have yielded very rich ore containing silver and a little gold. As Slater Bob put it: 'There was Queen Elizabeth and her Dutchies here, and a mort of folk after that, scratting and scratting . . . and the best of it still to find . . .' This was the legend behind the pinch of dust that the doomed young soldier showed Slater Bob before he disappeared, the legend of 'gold in t'fell' which turned the Amazon pirates and the Swallow explorers into prospectors.

On the way down Wetherlam, just below the path along the Birk Fell shoulder, I found Birk Hause Mine. It had some luridly coloured rocks among the spoil from its tunnel, orange and rust-stained quartz with bright smears of what I was sure the next geologist I met would tell me was 'fool's gold' on it. Still, it looked good enough gold to me. I picked up a hunk for each of the children, and then went on down, circling the bleak peat bog and getting back to the main mine at the top of Tilberthwaite Gill.

The footpath on the south side of the stream led me down to Penny Rigg Quarry, where I peered down the tunnel opening to the Tilberthwaite Deep Level. Holland's sketch map showed a plan of the working, with the cavern where Slater Bob hammered away some 250 ft from the entrance. There have been roof-falls in the Deep Level, and there may be more. It is certainly not possible to get out at the other end any more, nor was it ever a question of a straightforward walk. There would have been shafts to climb as well.

Wetherlam is no place for small children or inquisitive dogs. Some tunnels look safe enough, but both roofs and floors can be very dangerous. When prospecting, the miners let 'levels' into the hillside, and these seem to be safe, straight tunnels. Beware. Lower down the hillside there may well be another level. To link the two, shafts were driven downwards, often for several hundred feet. Wooden floors, deep in stone debris or even water, cover these shafts, and there is no guarantee at all that, having taken ten or twelve steps along

AS IF HE DID NOT KNOW THEY WERE THERE

a tunnel, the would-be prospector will not plunge down in an Alice-in-Wonderland type fall with no White Rabbit at the end of it. Every year serious accidents occur in such mine-workings. Walk High Topps with care. Leave cave exploration to the experts.

VI

Hot on the Trail

Towards the end of my fortnight, I went to see Titty Altounyan, who has spent many years near Coniston, partly at Lanehead, and partly in her present house overlooking the lake. Would she be as like the Titty in the books as Roger, Brigit and Taqui had suggested? I had seen a painting which her mother made of her as a little girl and gave to Arthur Ransome. He had kept it by him until he died. It certainly looked like the Titty of the stories, a character of whom Ransome was especially fond. Titty, with her dreams of being marooned 'like Ben Gunn', her brave clutching of the dowsing twig, her sorcery with the wax image of the great-aunt, is startlingly original and perhaps the best loved of all the characters. She has both the imagination to make her afraid and the courage to conquer her fears.

From the letters she had written to Ransome as a child, the real Titty sounded very like her fictional self. I had read them at Leeds. They were long letters, like the one Titty sends Commander Walker to ask if they can camp on Wild Cat Island, which is 'longer even than John's'. Here is part of one of them:

There was a native rowing boat near at hand, and at first Daddy and I thought we could rig it up and sail in it, but it wouldn't do, so we had to content ourselves with rowing in the native war canoe. Anyhow, we had a lovely bathe, though they were fishing that day, and the sharks *would* swim between my legs . . .

Roger can't swim yet, at least not without one leg on the bottom so if we had a shipwreck I don't know what would happen. I can swim, though I can't imagine how I swam with the telescope. The other day I tried putting both my hands above my head and swimming, but I only went under.

It was Titty who invited Ransome out to see what their life in Syria was like ('Mummy says that you should come and see what we are like now for yourself'). She used to climb the stairs to the room at the top of their house where he was working away on *Peter Duck*, and he would hold up his fingers to show her how many pages he had written. She helped him with the pictures for it, and today she is a painter in her own right.

When I showed these long-ago letters to Titty Altounyan, she couldn't remember writing them. She insisted that she was *not* like the Titty in the stories, not nearly so literary or so imaginative. In fact, she used to find it very difficult when people who knew of her connection with the Ransome books expected her to be like Ransome's Titty. I began to realize, as I talked to her, so like and yet not like Titty, how confusing such a situation must have been, particularly at an age when she had hardly begun to see herself as a person.

She had been very fond of the Ransomes, and sometimes stayed on her own with them at Low Ludderburn. When she was a few years older, she and Taqui had joined them for a sailing holiday on the Norfolk Broads.

I wasn't really very keen on sailing by then (she told me), but Taqui was. I do remember trying to be as Tittyish as possible. We were the boat that collected the post, and I thought of decorating all the letters with a special postmark as we brought them back from the post-office to wherever the rest of the fleet was moored. I called it the Whippet Post – that was the sort of boat we sailed, a

Whippet. I suppose I really did it just for Uncle Arthur's sake, not because I was like Titty.

Being a painter on the banks of Coniston Water would have been a good way for the fictional Titty to end up. But the real Titty had made me understand that it was a question of integrity, that a sensitive person might not like being dressed up like a paper doll in a set of clothes not of her choosing.

*

The last of the Lake books, *The Picts and the Martyrs*, was written at The Heald, a house on the eastern shore of Coniston Water into which the Ransomes moved in 1940 when they returned to the lake after six years in Suffolk. The Heald is set in a wood of its own which runs down to the lake shore. Ransome wrote in what he called his office, a separate building close to the house which has now been made into another house itself. The trees all around made it the right place for writing about the Picts' primitive house-keeping in the Dogs' Home. Evgenia thought it a very bad book, and glowered disapproval throughout its writing. Was Ransome's office literally the doghouse? Fortunately he finished the book despite her withering criticisms. His readers, on the other hand, were delighted to be back in the familiar world of the lake country, and Nancy is allowed to show how much sensitivity lies under her timber-shivering exterior. It is the shortest of the books, and also the funniest. Squashy Hat reappears, still very like Oscar Gnosspelius. 'He'd rather walk than sail,' says Nancy, 'but Uncle Jim says he's first rate on mountains.' Gnosspelius wrote to Ransome in 1933: 'My chief dislike of boats is due to their absurd slowness.'

The book is dedicated to Ransome's Aunt Helen, a 'Certificated First Class Aunt . . . not to be confused with Uncertificated Aunts like Nancy's and Peggy's.' She was herself a novelist, so I got hold of a few of her books to see if

Ransome had learnt anything from her. *Bess* and *Bats at Twilight* failed to grip me, but in *Josephine Crewe* I found a tomboyish heroine outsmarting her fellow guttersnipes at salvage in the London Docks in a distinctly Nancyish manner.

It was Aunt Helen who had stood by Ransome when, to his mother's dismay, he decided to become a writer instead of finishing his science course at the Yorkshire College. She visited him regularly, and it seems that she was particularly helpful when he was plotting *Picts*. I found a page in his notebook headed *Aunt Helen's Suggestion*; it was that the great-aunt should get lost while trying to catch out Nancy and Peggy, and that there should be a great hunt for her. It was the answer to a desperate earlier note by Ransome, 'Problem: what the dickens is the climax?' With his own brilliant improvement, that the great-aunt should end up on the houseboat and be saved by the Ds, it helped him to finish a book that he remained uncertain about until the end. It was aptly subtitled 'Not Welcome at All'.

The major new character in *Picts* was *Scarab*, the sailing dinghy which the Rio boatbuilders made for the Ds.

> She lay upside down on trestles, her bottom shiny with smooth black varnish, her sides gleaming gold in the sunshine that slanted through the open door.
>
> 'Is she only thirteen feet?' asked Dick. 'She looks much bigger.'
>
> 'She's as near the same as your boat as we could make her,' the old boatbuilder said to Nancy. 'That's what Mr Turner said was wanted. You'll be racing, I dare say.'

The model for *Scarab* was *Coch-y-bonddhu*, a sailing dinghy which Ransome had arranged for Crossfield's, the Arnside boatbuilders who originally built *Swallow*, to make for his friends the Renolds. A scarab is a type of salmon float, and coch-y-bonddhu is the name of a fishing fly. Charles Renold, a keen fisherman, never took to sailing, and Ransome kept the dinghy for himself. He sailed her at Pin Mill and in Secret Water, and then had her moved to Coniston Water when he and Evgenia bought The Heald. There she could have a little harbour of her own in front of the house. He was extremely fond of her, because she was so very like the old *Swallow* (except for the centreboard case, which was more like *Amazon/Mavis*). When he moved south again she had to be sold. She was bought by John Barnes, headmaster of a school in Arnside, and brother of the kind owner of my signalling station at Barkbooth, Sheila Caldwell.

Arnside seemed to keep cropping up. I drove south to the other side of the wide estuary which divides Lancaster from Lakeland to see if the boatbuilders who built *Swallow*, and so in a way started it all, were still there. Arnside is a tiny stone town which curls along the southern shores of the estuary. John Barnes, retired now, and his wife Dorothy told me all about *Coch-y-bonddhu* and the fun the family had had sailing her. Then we walked down to the boatyard. The Crossfield family are no longer running it, but it is still thriving. I saw the huge hull of a motor cruiser, a racy eighteen-footer, and the promising shell of a wooden canoe, which looked just right for Brigit Altounyan. The boat which I liked best was a small clinker-built sailing dinghy. About twelve foot long, she had a gaff-rig like *Swallow*. She wasn't new, and had once been tender to a Norwegian yacht.

'How much is she?' I asked.

'£320,' replied the boatbuilder. 'Complete.'

Rather more than Ernest Altounyan had paid back in 1928, I supposed. But there she was – adventure for the taking. I can still see her neat, cut-off bow, sturdy wooden thwarts, and fresh white paint.

*

Two weeks of exploring had given me lots of names to put on to the blank official map I had started with. The Octopus Lagoon, Kanchenjunga, High Topps, Holly Howe, Wild Cat Island, and its secret harbour, Darien, Cormorant Island, Horseshoe Cove, the Observatory, perhaps also Beckfoot, perhaps Swallowdale. Now the rest of the family were due to arrive, and I would find out what they thought of my progress. I swept away the heaps of papers, pictures and maps which had been carpeting the sitting-room, washed up for the first time in four days, and made up five more beds. Then I went into Bowness-on-Windermere and filled two large boxes with provisions. When my husband, Tom, and our four children arrived, the welcoming feast was a good one, if not quite as good as that which Captain Flint was able to get sent from Rio to the houseboat:

> There were ices, strawberry ones. There were parkin and bath buns and rock cakes and ginger nuts and chocolate biscuits. There were mountains of sandwiches to begin with. Then there was a cake with a paper cover over it. When the cover was lifted off, there was a picture of two little ships done in pink and white icing.
> 'The *Swallow* and the *Amazon*,' said Roger.
> 'That's what they're meant for,' said Captain Flint.

There was plenty to interest our four town children close by the house: the ford through the River Winster, the woods full of tiny daffodils, and the fine climbing rocks behind the house. But they were eager to see the first of the lakes, so we climbed Gummer's How to look down at Windermere. Tilly, Daisy and Ellen tackled the steep south face with Tom while I took Susanna, who was only four, round the gentler path to the east. We saw an adder sunning itself, climbed any tree that offered branches low enough, and eventually joined the advance party at the pillar that marks the top. Tilly thought that Blakeholme needed to be even bigger to be like Wild Cat Island, besides being farther out in the lake, and Daisy felt that Windermere was too long, and not wide enough. Everyone liked the snow-topped mountains. I pointed out Kanchenjunga, and we decided to go to Coniston and hunt for Swallowdale the next day. They thought I had been rather stupid not to look there in the first place.

'And can we meet Bridget?' asked Ellen.

'And find the Knickerbrockerbeaker?' said Susanna.

We got up early next day, and drove to Nibthwaite, parked the car and began test climbs and slides on the steep rocks just through the gate to the fell. We seemed to get very high very quickly. Ellen chose a fine boat-like collection of rocks for young Arthur's *Gondola*, and Susie peered with interest at a very dead sheep. At last, on the way down, Tilly gave a shout of triumph. I looked round to see her shooting down a very rough-looking sheet of stone, just above the track to Bethecar. The lumps on it turned out to be heather rather than rock, and they gave it a gentle cushioning that made it possible to slide down it very fast. I tore my trousers, but only slightly. There was no need to darn them.

When everyone had tried it out (several times) we went back into Nibthwaite to have a cup of coffee with Brigit and John. She was a little older than Ellen had expected, but could tell enough good stories about where Arthur Ransome used to play to make up for that. Tilly disappeared underneath his favourite bridge, helping Susie to find a footing on the bigger stones. Daisy and Ellen went off to inspect the boathouse, and try skimming stones across the lake.

Then we offered the children a choice – a long climb up Kanchenjunga and along the ridge to Wetherlam with Tom, or a march in search of Swallowdale with me. They all chose Swallowdale; it sounded easier going.

After leaving Tom at the foot of his mountain, we drove on along the west side of the lake to a car park on the Torver Beck, just past Beckstones on the A5084. We put on rubber boots and woollen caps, and set off upstream with a picnic basket and a puncheon of grog. When we had crossed the stepping stones we turned south along Mere Beck, a cheerful stream with good trees to climb and fine pools to fish. As we got higher on the moor, the beck deserted us, taking a sharp western bend to a pleasant little grassy clearing, but away from my goal, Beacon Hill. Three of us were for staying here, but we went on, the vision of Swallowdale ahead like a Holy Grail. Whipped by the wind, pursued by amiable cows, hopping from tussock to tussock through Stable Harvey Moss, we slogged on. Just as despair was beginning to set in,

THE CAMP IN SWALLOWDALE

Tilly pointed ahead with a whoop of excitement.

'The Watch Tower!'

There certainly was a huge, flat-topped rock ahead, all alone too and on the right side of the valley, which could be hidden behind it.

97

We stopped for lunch, confident that Swallowdale was just around the corner. Lunch helped progress for a while, but when the other side of the Watch Tower turned out to be swampy moor, our spirits fell. I looked at my maps again and compared Ransome's drawing with them. We needed to be much closer to the Beacon. I pointed up a steep hillside. Mutiny resulted.

'The Swallows and the Amazons ran across this moor two or three times a day,' I argued.

'We aren't the Swallows and Amazons,' said Daisy firmly.

'We're real children, not storybook ones,' added Ellen.

As a compromise, I suggested the easier path along the hillside. It was a little west of where I thought we ought to be, but it was a gently climbing sheeptrack, which made gaining height very easy. Eventually it led to another track, boldly marked on my map as the Cumbria Way. My heart sank. Could Swallowdale have become a well-trodden national footpath? The track levelled out in a wide valley, with a peaty tarn speckled with small islands. The expedition sat down and declared itself satisfied. I looked at the scree to the east. Just over it, my map told me, there were at least two possible streams for Swallowdale, under Beacon Hill as drawn by Ransome. I looked at the expedition, which had begun to hunt crocodiles in the Mississippi delta of the tarn. There was no question of them climbing any farther.

Suddenly, an incredibly generous solution occurred to me. I would leave the discovery of Swallowdale for readers of this book to make for themselves. With Arthur Ransome's map and all my failures to help them, it ought to be an easy matter. No Ransomite likes to be spoonfed, I reasoned. I just hope that one day someone lets me know where it is.

*

The next day, it began to rain. And the next day, and the next. Ransome's weather had deserted us. The children played board games, read books and occasionally went outside and got soaking wet collecting wood. I taught Tilly and Daisy Miss Milligan's patience, the game Captain Flint plays in *Peter Duck*. Brigit said that they always used to play racing demon as children – very noisily.

Miss Milligan's Patience (two packs required)

Deal eight cards in a row. Play aces to the centre of the table, and build on them in ascending suit order to the kings. The cards in the layout are arranged in descending sequence of alternate colour. A space may only be filled by a king, with or without a sequence on it. When all moves have been made in the first row of eight, deal another eight cards, slightly overlapping the cards in the first row, and filling any spaces. No card can be built on to the aces or the layout until all eight new cards have been dealt. Play continues, making moves after each row of eight cards have been dealt, until the pack is exhausted. Sequences must be moved intact. When the whole pack has been dealt, but not before, if a card at the bottom of a column blocks the run of a sequence, it may be taken into the hand and held in reserve until more moves let the player find a place for it in the layout. This is known as waiving, and though it may be repeated as often as the player wishes, only one card at a time may be waived.

It looked as if the rest of my plans would have to be scrapped. We never hired a motor launch from the boatyard in Bowness Bay to take a picnic to the islands. We didn't follow the Brantwood nature trail to spot old charcoal-burners' pitsteads in The Heald's woods. We didn't see a hound trail. We didn't tremble at the mouths of mines ('I was glad about that,' said Tom, who had seen them on his way down Wetherlam). We didn't climb Kanchenjunga in easy stages. But we will one day, at a quiet time of year, now that we know that Ransome's places are still much as he left them.

What about his people? I had told the children all I had found out. They had met Brigit themselves, and liked the sound of the rest of the Altounyan family.

'In a way, those children giving Arthur Ransome the idea for *Swallows and Amazons* was just like Titty finding Captain Flint's book for him,' said Tilly slowly. 'I think you're wrong about *Mixed Moss* being like his *Autobiography*. I always thought it was really *Swallows and Amazons*.'

She had a point. The way Captain Flint said thank you to the Swallows for finding the book that was his first bestseller was to pay for *Swallow*'s repairs after her wreck in *Swallowdale*. Ransome thanked the children he knew by taking a little dinghy out to Syria for them, and by remaining an 'Uncle' to them for the rest of his life. They grew up rather too fast to stay the right age for his stories, but he found plenty of other eager and 'web-footed' young friends to take on capsizing parties and feast with grog, and he adapted their adventures in later stories.

'Nancy is still a bit of a muddle,' said Daisy. 'Is she Taqui or is she Barbara Collingwood or is she Georgina Rawdon-Smith? There seem to be too many people being her.'

Peggy was just as much of a muddle, but they thought she was such a shadowy character anyway that she didn't matter so much.

'I think he put her in so that Nancy would have someone to boss about; so she wouldn't just be alone,' said Tilly.

'Nancy bosses everyone about,' said Ellen. 'Even Arthur Ransome. Putting messages into the books herself, I mean.'

'But he did like her, didn't he?' said Daisy. 'She helped him with the pictures, and had such a lot of good ideas. She sounds like a really good friend of his, I think.'

I thought about a book written by William Canton, an older friend of Arthur Ransome's. It was called *The Invisible Playmate*. Perhaps the answer to the mystery was that he had made Nancy up to be the perfect tomboy girl that he had never met in reality, using things he liked about several girls he knew. Then he grew so fond of her that she did become real – to him. But the only visible shape he could give her was to name his favourite boat, 'the best little ship I ever sailed in,' after her: *Nancy Blackett*.

VII

Better Drowned than Duffers

E.F. Knight's slim blue book, *Sailing*, was consulted by both Dick Callum and John Walker. It was also the book from which Arthur Ransome himself learnt to handle a boat, once he had been introduced to sailing by Robin, Barbara and Dora Collingwood in the first *Swallow*. In its opening pages there is a sentence which sums up perfectly Ransome's experiences with the boats he owned himself: 'Some men – good sailors too – never succeed in mating themselves with the right craft, but are perpetually building or buying and selling again without satisfying themselves.' What were those boats like, I wanted to know, and did any of them appear in his stories?

When Ransome was living on the shores of the Baltic Sea after his escape from Russia with Evgenia, his nearest town and shopping centre was Reval, built as a fortress on a rock.

One looks down over a wide bay, with the green wooded island of Nargon on one side of it, a long promontory on the other, and far out beyond the bay a horizon of open sea. I do not believe that a man can look out from that rock and ever be wholly happy until he has got a boat of his own. I could not, and on each of my trips to Reval I walked around the harbour looking for something that would float, and had a mast and sail.

One day he found a long, shallow boat, with a mast, a

101

square transom, and a short iron bowsprit. Her ballast was a collection of large boulders, and her price £10 (1920 money). He bought her, on condition that she would be ready to sail the next day, and went off with a sea-captain friend to choose a compass. He was lucky enough to find a little pocket prismatic compass made by Negretti & Zambra which he kept all his life – it is still on his desk in the Abbot Hall Museum at Kendal.

The boat's maiden voyage, under a much-patched lugsail and staysail, took place in an almost dead calm the next day. 'There came a breath of wind,' wrote Ransome, 'and slowly, so slowly that we there and then christened her *Slug*, she moved out into the middle of the bay, and we were looking at the rock of Reval from the sea as I had often promised we should.' He almost lost her straight away. The wind dropped completely, and he decided to jump overboard for a swim and to 'admire my lovely command'. The wind got up again, and off swept *Slug*, with Evgenia, who had never sailed before, shrieking at him to catch her up. With a superhuman effort, Ransome did so, only to find that he couldn't climb over her steep sides. Luckily, he managed to pull himself in over the bow by gripping the bowsprit.

Undismayed, the two of them set off the next day for a forty-mile voyage along the coast to get home to Lahepe. *Slug* rode out a squall in fine style, although a passing cutter 'flashed past with lee scuppers under'. They anchored in the dark (like the Swallows returning from the Amazon boathouse) and woke to find themselves surrounded by rocks and friendly seals. Perhaps the largest, who looked over the side of the boat 'with shining head and dripping whiskers . . . like an elderly business man bathing at Margate', was in Ransome's mind when the Swallows spotted 'George', the seal in *Secret Water*.

A few hours later, they were at Lahepe Bay, and waded triumphantly ashore, holding their luggage high above their heads to keep it dry. 'A ridiculous beginning,' reflected Ransome, to take an open boat and novice crew tacking for some sixty miles down a coast they did not know. A letter

which he wrote shortly afterwards in July 1920 to Barbara
Collingwood showed how little he knew himself at the time.
It also showed that he was determined to learn more, and fast.

My dear Barbara,

First voyage satisfactorily accomplished . . . I had to
work entirely on what I remembered of Robin's instructions. But one thing he never taught me, and that was how to
heave to in a wind, and keep more or less in one place without
handling the sails. I know the thing is done by fixing the sails
and the tiller someway or other, but no amount of rule of
thumb experience arrived at the desired result. I shall be
much obliged for detailed instructions, if possible with
diagram on this point.

The rig of the boat is not quite the same as *Swallow*'s or
Jamrach's. The gaff? (the stick at the top of the mainsail)
projected in front of the mast. The boom is as per *Swallow*.
There is also a triangular foresail? jib, called hereabouts the
cleaver.

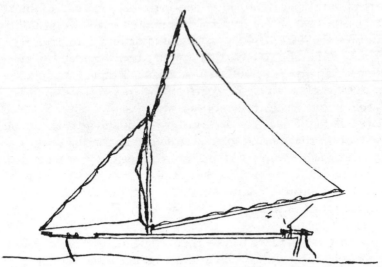

She is I think 18 feet long. She was built about a hundred
years ago, but she practically does not leak at all.

103

All her rigging is rotten. Ditto her sails, which are made of something suspiciously like old sheets. We've spent the day in repairs. In the course of the repairs arose about five hundred technical questions for Robin or Ernest, and neither of these Nestors are on hand. I have with trepidation but apparent success, taken out the rope that howks the main sail up, and put it back tother end on, because it had a knot at one place, which made it impossible to lower it altogether. Further I have developed what seems to me to be rather a shady trick of tying the low corner of the mainsail to the thwart beside the mast. Nothing else to tie it to.

A screw with a ring to it probably meant for that purpose came out bodily, suggesting rottenness in the mast, which, for peace of mind, I have to refrain from investigating. E. has patched the mainsail with tablecloth, and talks of grey paint. She says she prefers boats to fishing, and has already learnt to sail the *Slug* in a calm.

I think that unless some accident puts an end to our experiments, another month of Baltic cruising on a minute scale should bring us on a long way in the practical part of the business. But I fairly yearn for Robin, and curse every few minutes the many hours of possible sailing I missed at Coniston. I ought to have tied myself to *Swallow*, and slept on her, and gone out with her whenever Robin descended from on high to make her perform her mysteries. Then I should know a little more about it . . .

The Baltic, I may say, has one great advantage over our own seas, in that there is no tide. So if you hit a sandbank with your keel once, you can be sure of hitting it again at any hour of the day. Rocks do not play bo-peep with you. There are hundreds and thousands of them but where they are there they remain, and the wise sailor takes off his hat to them as he passes.

I have got a pretty good German chart of 1908, showing the whole of the gulf of Finland . . . It has little miniature pictures of all the lighthouses, so that you can recognise them by day. Enormous fun. I have now made the acquaintance of four of them.

The awful thing about open boat cruising is that one gets absolutely no rest. There is no cabin, no means of sleeping out of the sun, and for grub one has either to land, an unwelcome and risky operation, or else do without a fire and exist on sandwiches. I have absolutely made up my mind to get a boat for singlehanded sailing with a cabin, and with everything thought out wilily to make her working easy. Ratchet reefing for example. Everything fixed for comfort so that one could really live on board, which in an open boat like the *Slug* is impossible. On our thirty-six-hour trip, I had only four hours of v. uncomfortable sleep in the bottom of the boat, while at anchor.

Now please, if possible, get answers to some of the questions in this letter . . . particularly about heaving to. I know that by some trick it is possible to fix up the boat so that she will look after herself, and leave you free, for example to mend a rope, or to eat a meal.

After *Slug* had sunk twice on her moorings in Lahepe Bay, the Ransomes found themselves something more of a ship. *Kittiwake* was two feet shorter than *Slug*, but she had a little cabin. As there were no boat-builders who would make them a dinghy in Reval, they asked a firm of undertakers to make one, arguing that if they could make coffins they could also make boats.

The result was an odd triangular craft which was very wobbly. 'If I shifted my pipe from one side of my mouth to the other, I never knew what might happen,' Ransome wrote home. Evgenia put some new mattresses on *Kittiwake*'s 'horribly narrow' bunks, made orange curtains for her portholes, and fitted out the galley. For all these home comforts, *Kittiwake* was never very seaworthy. 'She heeled over to her cabin-top, even with two reefs in her sail.' More ballast improved her a little, but she was too cramped to live in for any length of time. A fifty-mile voyage to Baltic Port took them far longer than Ransome had estimated. First there was too much wind, then too little, and he had to spend twenty-five hours at the tiller. 'I went ashore to book rooms in the little hotel kept by the harbourmaster, and fell asleep with my head on the table.' John Walker would do the same after his all-night crossing to Holland in *We Didn't Mean to Go to Sea*.

> John felt his eyes closing. He opened them and looked all round him. They closed again. His head felt somehow much heavier than usual. He propped it with a hand . . . with both hands. Nothing would keep it up. Down it went, down . . . down. Daddy reached out just in time to move John's plate before he dipped his hair in it. John had fallen asleep with his head on the table.
>
> 'Skipper's been a long time on the bridge,' said his father quietly.
>
> 'That's what happened to Jim Brading when he came to supper,' said Roger.
>
> 'He'd sailed all the way from Dover,' said Titty.
>
> 'And you've sailed a lot further than that,' said Daddy.

It was a fine summer for sailing. The Ransomes had the use of the whale-boats of a friendly British steamer, and of the harbourmaster's skiff. They met Otto Eggers, a famous boat designer, who had lost his Reval boatyard because of the Russian Revolution. He designed a fishing dinghy for them, to replace the coffin, and then they began to draw up a dream boat, 'big and comfortable enough to live in for months on end, and fit to be sailed to England if and when we wanted to do so'. Later in the summer they moved south to Riga, where they found a boat-builder to make the dinghy. He did it so well that Ransome felt he could be trusted with *Racundra*. The blueprints for both *Racundra* and the little dinghy, signed by Otto Eggers, were at the very bottom of Captain Flint's trunk in the Leeds library. I unfolded the huge sheets of blue, linen-weave paper and studied *Racundra*'s lines with respect. For this was the ship that set Ransome on course at last. She was his escape from politics and journalism towards things much closer to his heart. The success of the book he wrote about her, *Racundra's First Cruise*, gave him

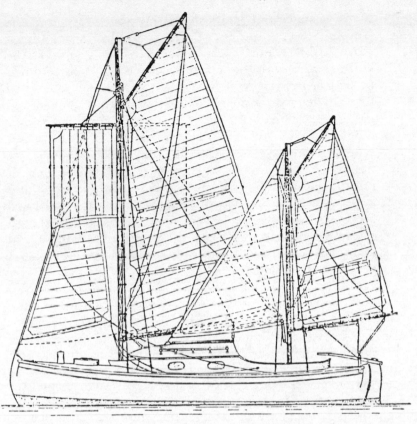

RACUNDRA

the confidence to chance *Swallows and Amazons.*

'I took a deep breath and signed the contract to build her, determined to do enough writing to pay for it,' he wrote. All winter he watched her being built, enjoying the cosy hospitality of the Riga Yacht Club, which turned to ice-yachting when it was too frozen for boats. Next summer, impatient to finish her off, Ransome took her round to the little harbour where they kept the dinghy, and put her in the hands of an old sailor called Captain Sehmel, who was in charge of the harbour.

107

Many years ago he had sailed from Southampton in the famous *Sunbeam* of Lord Brassey. He had spent fifteen years of his youth in Australia. He had shared in the glorious runs of the old teaclippers. He had been a seaman in the *Thermopylae*, which he called the *Demooply*, and had raced in her against the *Kutuzak* in which odd Russianized name I recognised the *Cutty Sark* . . . He took care of my dinghy as if she were an ocean liner, made her a padded wharf to preserve her varnish, and spoke of her quick passages across the little lake as if she was a clipper returning round the Horn. He and I became friends, and long before *Racundra* was finished, knowing that I planned a voyage to England, he went to see her in her shed, and returning, begged me to take him with me. 'I am an old man,' he said, 'and I should like once more to go to sea before it is too late.'

Reread the first pages of *Peter Duck*, and its description of the old sailor 'with a fringe of a white beard around a face that was as brown and wrinkled as a walnut', who watched the *Wild Cat* making ready to go foreign, to blue water, and 'wished he could go to sea once more, and make another voyage before it was too late'. Captain Sehmel was not only the star of *Peter Duck*, he was also the Ancient Mariner who sailed with Ransome and the Cook (Evgenia, naturally) in *Racundra's First Cruise*. Captain Sehmel completed Ransome's sailing education on that cruise, just as Peter Duck guided Captain Flint's judgment when necessary.

What was *Racundra* like? Ransome described her in loving detail at the end of his book. She was just under thirty foot long, twelve foot in beam, and drew three-foot six without her centreboard, seven-foot six with it. She was a ketch, so she had two masts, and normally sailed with staysail, mainsail and mizzen. She could carry a great deal more canvas, but Ransome always liked to feel that he could sail his boats single-handed. So she had no bowsprit, and the end of the mizzen boom could be reached from the tiller. Her 'chief glory' was her enormous cabin. Ransome had a comfortable writing desk a yard square, with a chart drawer and a special cupboard for his typewriter below it. Above was a bookshelf, 'high enough to take the *Nautical Almanac*, the *Admiralty Pilot*, Dixon Kemp and Norie's *Epitome* and *Tables*'.

In 1924, Ransome left the Baltic for good and brought Evgenia back to England. Originally, he had planned to return to Riga for *Racundra*, and to write a second cruise book. He had even gathered some of the material, including a description of a waterspout they had seen near Riga that would come in useful for *Peter Duck*. As it turned out, ill-health and lack of money forced him to sell *Racundra* in order to pay for Low Ludderburn, their new home in the Lake District. She was bought by Adlard Coles, who cruised round the Baltic in her, and then brought her back to England. His book, *Close-Hauled*, tells the story. Although *Racundra* is called *Annette II* in the book, her name was not really changed, and a close look at the photographs in Coles's book reveals the truth.

Racundra's next long-term owner was J.M. Baldock, the Hampshire M.P. Then she suffered several rapid changes of owner, and ended up shabby and uncared for in Tangiers, owned by a Spanish company. However, her adventures were not quite over.

Rodney Pickering, an adventurer after Ransome's own heart, started ocean sailing when he was only seventeen. In 1976 he recognized *Racundra* in Tangier, and scraped up enough money to buy her. Gradually he restored her to her old ample glory, even to the original now rather old-fashioned gaff-rig, which an earlier owner had made Bermudan. He sailed *Racundra* to Caracas in 1978, and reported her in letters 'a fine sea-going boat'. He was planning to bring her back to Britain via the West Indies, but disaster overtook him. Sailing single-handed about ninety miles off the Venezuelan coast, he hit a reef. Pickering managed to save a few fittings, but had to abandon the ship which he had made his home. 'When he wrote about the experience of losing her on the reef,' his uncle told me, 'he merely said he felt like a snail without its shell.'

Worse was to come. Rodney Pickering and his cousin set

out in a catamaran for Martha's Vineyard, New England, in June 1982, 'almost certainly bound for England'. Neither has been heard of since. But there is a mystery to be solved. In April 1982, a long article on *Racundra* appeared in the magazine, *Yachting World*. It reported that she was in Santa Lucia in the West Indies, and was owned by a Rodney Fingleton. The boat photographed there looks like the broad-beamed *Racundra* in some ways, but she is Bermuda-rigged, and has a quite different cabin top and well from that shown in the original drawings and early photographs of her. Could her hull have been salvaged? Perhaps, like a cat with nine lives, *Racundra* is still afloat.

Ransome spent the next ten years without a boat. He sailed *Swallow* on the Lakes, and bigger cabin yachts on the Broads. 'I did not feel I had the right to take my wife to sea, knowing that at any moment I might turn into a useless passenger,' he wrote. But a major operation in 1933 made him feel that he might at last be able to sail seriously again. He convalesced after the operation in the little port of St Mawes in Cornwall (the very place into which *Shining Moon* sails triumphantly at the end of *Missee Lee*), and just across the Carrick Roads from Falmouth, where Commander Walker taught John the sailing essentials which helped him get *Goblin* across the North Sea on his own.

The stay in St Mawes was the idea of Herbert Hanson, secretary to the Cruising Association, and a great friend of Ransome's. *Missee Lee* was dedicated to Hanson, and Ransome nearly bought the massive barge *Industry* which Hanson was having refitted. He liked her lines, and her 'colossal' cabin, but was doubtful about her size. '46 feet sounds nothing, but when you stand up inside it, among these ribs, it is like being in a cathedral. And when you look at her from the outside, up on the hard, it's like looking at a prehistoric ten-times-magnified hippopotamus.'

Fortunately, he did not buy her. She was far too big for a man so prone to sudden illness, although he was to see her often on the East Coast, renamed *Deerfoot*, and lived in all year round by a colourful master mariner known as 'Bo'sun

Walker'. Instead, he sailed on the Falmouth coast in Hanson's yacht *Ianthe*, and half-planned a story set in St Mawes with its creeks and pine-covered hills and gardens and palm trees.

It was the hope of sailing larger boats which led to the Ransomes' move from Low Ludderburn to Broke Farm, at Levington in Suffolk. Across the River Orwell from Broke Farm was the friendly little East Coast port of Pin Mill, the very place where the Swallows are pottering about in a borrowed dinghy at the opening of *We Didn't Mean to Go to Sea*.

'What's written on that buoy?' said Titty.

'*Goblin*,' said Roger. 'Funny name for a boat. I wonder where she is?'

'There's a boat coming up the river now,' said John, 'but she may be going right up to Ipswich . . .'

'Her sails are a lovely colour,' said Titty.

A little white cutter with red sails was coming in towards the moored boats. Someone was busy on her foredeck. As they watched, they saw the tall red mainsail crumple and fall in great folds on the top of the cabin.

In every detail *Goblin* was the *Nancy Blackett*, a thirty-foot long, seven-ton cutter that Ransome bought in 1934. They were the same right down to the registration number that Jim Brading shouts to the Harwich harbourmaster, 'no. 16856.' She had been built by Hillyard's of Littlehampton in 1931, and was originally called *Spindrift*. Her next owner changed that to *Electron*, but Ransome called her *Nancy Blackett*, feeling that 'but for Nancy I should never have been able to buy her'. He sailed her round from Poole in Dorset to Pin Mill in a steadily increasing gale. The coastguard who saw her off the Needles warned the lifeboat to stand by, but Ransome and his crew, Peter Tisbury, arrived safely, 'expressed suitable surprise' at this concern, 'and made a very rough wet stow before settling down to hog'. The voyage proved *Nancy*'s quality: 'a wonderful little boat and so

111

comfortable that a man can spend many months on end in her'.

She was very easy to handle, and had roller reefing, so it was not impossible that the Walker children, with their good sense and seamanship, got her safely to Flushing. Here she is at her finest, returning from a night in Hamford Water in 1936:

> With the storm sails she was quite happy, and fairly flew, big waves picking her up, and she riding the top of them in a flurry of white foam until they passed her and she slipped down to be picked up by the next. It was really gorgeous. We did not see any other yachts on the whole passage, just one steamship and two barges, which looked very fine indeed. The three of us, the two big Thames barges and my little *Nancy*, all came storming round the Naze together.

Ransome had five happy years with *Nancy Blackett*, years which gave him *We Didn't Mean to Go to Sea* and *Secret Water*. In later years he was to kick himself for selling her, 'the best little boat I ever had'. But Evgenia found the galley cramped, and Ransome hoped that a larger boat would make her more willing to sail with him. They had become good friends with the Pin Mill boat-builder Harry King, and it was tempting to think of designing another boat. Plans to build *Selina King* began and, when she was finished, *Nancy* was sold to a Ransome enthusiast called Reginald Russell, who named his house Blackett Cottage and kept the boat on the East Coast for eight years.

After three more owners, she was bought by William and Eunice Bentley in 1966, and they still own her. I went up to Scarborough to see her while she was being refitted. We sat in her cabin and talked about her. The Bentleys seemed to know *We Didn't Mean to Go to Sea* backwards.

'You know when the harbourmaster in Flushing asks John for her tonnage? And it says, "John knew by heart the figures carved on the main beam down in the cabin"? Well, there they are.'

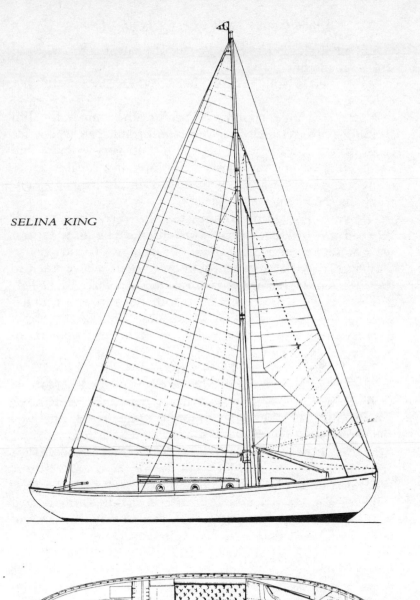

SELINA KING

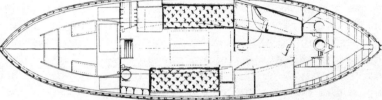

Sure enough, under several coats of paint, the tonnage can still be made out.

'And there's still a stove here, where Susan did her cooking.'

There are huge cupboards behind the bunks for Jim Brading's tins of stores, and four comfortable berths, one for each of the Swallows. The cabin felt very roomy and high-ceilinged, and the whole little ship had a capable air, as if she was game for any adventure that might happen along. Very like Nancy herself, in fact.

'We've had some marvellous times in her,' Eunice said. 'We did try for Holland once, just after we bought her, but we got caught in a force nine gale and my friend was so seasick that we had to turn back! Since then, we've stuck to the East Coast. It's amazing how many people know her. Whenever we go into a new port, someone turns up who has seen her before, or who knew Ransome. She's an incredibly popular little boat. They're always taking photographs of her.'

'Does she still have red sails?' I asked.

'She *should* have. But the sailmaker got it wrong, and made a white one. So her jib is red and her mainsail's white now, which looks a bit funny. I thought about dyeing it, but I decided it would just fade.'

Instead of being painted white, *Nancy Blackett* now has a green hull (like the *Wild Cat*) but for all the colour changes she was still her old self, and obviously in very good hands.

There are exact details of *Selina King*, Ransome's next boat, in Uffa Fox's *Thoughts on Yachts and Yachting*, a series of portraits of particularly interesting boats. A nine-ton cutter, thirty-six feet long, she was even bigger than *Racundra*, but careful thought was put into making her easy to handle. 'She is easier than *Nancy*, in many ways,' Ransome wrote to his mother. He planned a book about her building, and the cruises he hoped to have in her, but the outbreak of war and his worsening health combined against him. After only a handful of short voyages around the East Coast, he laid her up in Oulton Broad in September 1939, exactly a year after she was first launched. Because of the war, the Ransomes moved back up to the Lake District. By the time it was over, Ransome was over sixty years old, and often unwell. 'I am giving up my big ship on doctor's orders and am hoping to replace her by a much smaller, easier-run vessel, a sort of marine bathchair for my old age,' he wrote to a friend. In February 1946 he paid *Selina King* a sad last visit, and found that her keel and garboards were completely dried out. By March 1946 she was sold, although Ransome had only one season of cruises in her. She sailed on the south coast until 1963, when she was taken to Bermuda, her present home.

The Pin Mill boat-builder, Harry King, set to work again, this time to build *Peter Duck*, twenty-eight feet long and ketch-rigged so that none of her sails would be too much for Ransome to handle. Inevitably, he found her a comedown after *Selina King*, but like all the boats he sailed she was very attractive. However, Ransome only sailed in her for a couple of years. The war had destroyed his old way of life at Pin Mill. Many of the boys he had taken aboard as crews were killed in action, and I suspect that that sense of loss was one of the reasons that the Ransomes moved north yet again in 1948, after only three years in London.

I went to see *Peter Duck* at Woodbridge, and her present owner, Mrs Jones, told me how full of character she was. The Jones family had been concerned with her building, and bought her themselves in 1957, so she has had fewer owners than any of Ransome's other boats. She inspired a class of her own, of which forty-five were built between 1959 and 1963. The class design had an extra plank, and the cabin roof was carried forward of the mainmast. This gave more headroom but made the boats look a little lumpy. Mrs Jones feels that they lack the elegance of the original *Peter Duck*.

'She's a sea-kindly little boat,' she said. 'She really comes into her own in a smart breeze. I sometimes think we ought to sell her, but I can never quite bear to part with her. She's really one of the family now.'

Ransome was sixty-three when he sold *Peter Duck*. Only three years later he and Evgenia moved south yet again, and commissioned *Lottie Blossom* from David Hillyard's boatyard at Littlehampton, the boat-builders who had made *Nancy Blackett*. There are still people at Hillyard's who remember him coming down to watch her grow. The first *Lottie Blossom* was a standard twenty-four-foot Hillyard sloop with a central cockpit. The Ransomes decided that two cabins were unnecessary, and had her rebuilt with an aft cockpit, a large central cabin and a small forepeak. She was also equipped with the usual writing desk so that Ransome could work, as he loved to do, while cruising. Her name was that of P.G. Wodehouse's heroine in *The Luck of the Bodkins*. Lottie was an accomplished smuggler, who kept a small alligator in her handbag to discourage Customs men. P.G. Wodehouse wrote to Ransome to thank him for the compliment, and added that *The Luck of the Bodkins* was his own favourite book.

I noticed a photograph in Ransome's album of the *Mary Helen*, and it was clear that she and *Lottie Blossom* sometimes sailed together. The *Mary Helen*'s owner then, Mary Helen Tew, still sails her, and remembers the Ransomes well. She wrote me a letter describing how they listened to the Coronation broadcast in 1953 together at Beaulieu in Hampshire. Ransome kept *Lottie Blossom* in Chichester Harbour, and used to sail to France in her. 'We passed him going north a few miles out of Cherbourg on our way in, and when we met up later in Beaulieu heard that they had had quite a dusting in a storm, and regretted that we had not been in earlier and been together in Cherbourg.'

Ransome and Mrs Tew sat on the Royal Cruising Club Committee together. 'Have you noticed that the burgee on *Goblin* in *We Didn't Mean to Go to Sea* belongs to the Royal Cruising Club?' she asked me. 'I think that one of the reasons that his books are so fascinating is that he always wrote about what he knew and had experienced.'

Lottie Blossom had to be sold in 1954. At seventy, Ransome came to terms with the truth. His sailing days were over, but he could turn to his second great love, fishing. *Lottie* herself still flourishes, kept by Christopher Barlow in Chichester

Harbour, just as Ransome did. He and his family are keen Ransome readers, and are delighted to own a boat with such a history. *Lottie Blossom* will be making trips to the Channel Islands and France with her bookshelves stocked, just as they used to be by Ransome, with Joshua Slocum, E.F. Knight, *Racundra's First Cruise* and the rest. She has a larger jib than originally supplied, but otherwise she is just as she used to be, a plucky, solid little ship.

What do Ransome's boats tell us about him? He was an excellent designer of boats, but never quite satisfied with what he had. Fate decreed that while he was healthy enough to be an ambitious sailor – one of his favourite books was Joshua Slocum's *Sailing Alone Round the World* – he did not have the money to do so, and that when he was rich enough to have boats built to order he was not healthy enough to make ambitious voyages. His frustration was his readers' gain. In his books he sails, as Captain Flint, over the oceans he longed to cross. I felt that he should have been content to keep the *Nancy Blackett*, the boat that seemed to fit him so well. Perhaps, in the end, he went back to her. Before I left *Nancy*'s cabin, Eunice Bentley had told me a strange story.

'When we first looked at the *Nancy Blackett*, a friend of ours went inside her and then shot out again, really fast.

' "There's been someone smoking a pipe down there," he said, "and I hate tobacco." '

'Well, we bought her, and we scrubbed out the bilges, and repainted her, and varnished her. Now, no one in our family smokes, but it still sometimes happens. Just occasionally, there'll be this really strong smell of pipe tobacco. We think we've got a ghost. A nice friendly one, though. There's nothing creepy about *Nancy*.'

VIII

Coots and Foreigners

Even in Arthur Ransome's day, the Norfolk Broads were crowded with holidaymakers. *Coot Club* is carefully set after the Easter rush and *The Big Six* takes place at the beginning of autumn, when fishermen's thoughts start turning to pike. Fifty years later it takes more extreme measures to avoid the rush, which was why the children and I found ourselves hiring a boat at George Smith's Wroxham boatyard in February. To my shame she was not one of the *Teasel* look-alikes, *Jasmine* or *Daffodil*, which can still be rented through Blakes at Wroxham. Instead, we were travelling in Hullabaloo-style:

> A big motor cruiser had turned the corner above the Ferry and was thundering up the river with a huge gramophone open and playing on the roof of the forecabin. Two gaudily dressed women were lying beside it, and three men were standing in the well between the cabins. All three were wearing yachting-caps. One was steering and the other two were using binoculars and seemed to be searching the banks as the cruiser came upstream at a tremendous pace.
>
> 'They're looking for the *Dreadnought*,' whispered Tom.

So were we, in a bulbous six-berth cruiser called *Glitterwake*. Instead of the *Margoletta*'s gramophone there was a colour television aerial on the roof, and 'gaudily-dressed' was hardly

HULLABALOOS!

the right description of the bo'sun and me, muffled up to our
ears in scarves and puffy anoraks. The bo'sun was Jane Jones,
an old friend and sailing enthusiast who had come to crew.
She told us stories of sailing to Holland, and through
Holland, following the canals and rivers to 'meres' much

119

larger than the meres of Norfolk. Although she too itched to sail, we had decided that the children would be better off sheltering from the freezing February winds in *Glitterwake*'s roomy, centrally-heated cabin. Susanna, after all, cannot swim yet, even with one foot on the bottom.

I knew that there would be no guessing at geography on this cruise. We could easily use the endpaper maps of *Coot Club* instead of the holidaymakers' map which the boatyard had thoughtfully provided. Our plan was to nose through the rivers, dykes and meres in the wake of the *Teasel*, the *Titmouse* and the *Death and Glory*, but as we puttered along, rereading the books in the steamy cabin, I began to realize that they had much more to them than geographical accuracy. *Coot Club* describes in detail all the traditional Broadland craft, from the slim racing-dinghy, *Flash*, to the splendid wherry, *Sir Garnet*. *The Big Six* gives descriptions of eel-catching, fishing, and everyday life in the little Broadland villages, which show that Ransome knew their history very well.

When did his interest in this watery world east of Norwich start? It is difficult to be certain. He refers to a holiday spent one winter 'in the far distant past', on a wherry fishing for pike. He sailed a good deal with Ernest Altounyan ('Commander Walker') when he was a young man, and mentions in a letter that Altounyan was 'a great Broads sailor and has a library of Broads books'. Perhaps it was Altounyan who introduced him to Norfolk. His letters to Ransome from Syria are full of comparisons between the lagoons and reedy swamps of Antioch and those of Norfolk. Once he even asked Ransome to bring out the hull of a wherry with him, so that it could be used as a base for exploration from dinghies.

The first cruise on the Broads which Ransome logged was in late April 1931, when he and Evgenia took the *Welcome* (not a barge, but a small una-rigged cabin yacht with two berths) from the Herbert Wood's boatyard at Potter Heigham, and a friend, Ted Scott (then editor of the *Manchester Guardian*) hired her sister ship *Winsome* with his son Richard. There were details

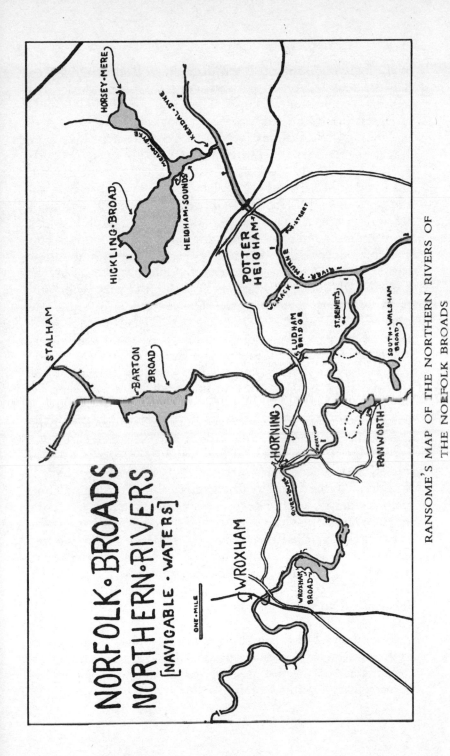

RANSOME'S MAP OF THE NORTHERN RIVERS OF
THE NORFOLK BROADS

in the log which will sound familiar to *Coot Club* readers. They sailed across Barton Broad and were 'nearly run down by a motor-cruiser while tacking'. They also admired a 22lb pike in a glass case at the Pleasure Boat Inn, at Hickling.

The next cruise (in early May, 1933) was with his neighbours from the Lake District, the Kelsalls of Barkbooth. Colonel Kelsall was still signal-happy, and Ransome noted in his log that he was 'very sick that our yeoman of signals was not up to his job'. Dick Kelsall remembers the flags running up and down the masts of their *Welcome* and the Ransomes' slightly larger *Fairway*, using the international code which Evgenia had not then mastered. But the Cook made good over quanting (the Norfolk term for punting). 'Evgenia did some neat work with the quant. *Welcome* did very well in the narrows, nearly catching us, but she could not equal our quant.' When they ran on to the mud, 'the heroic cook set to in the dinghy, and with me quanting a little and shifting my 16-stone bow to stern, got her out into the fairway'.

They saw a 'fine business wherry sailing through', and moored for the night by Horning Hall, as did the *Teasel*. There was a boy 'setting nightlines and eel traps' near by. A friend towed them through Yarmouth to Breydon Water and the southern rivers, and they sailed up to Norwich and down to Oulton Broad. There they moored in the yacht harbour and talked to the harbourmaster about buying boats. I wondered if they'd had hot baths for a shilling using 'oilskins for dressing-gowns', like the crew of the *Teasel* after the storm over Oulton.

Farther along the River Waveney, at Beccles, they moored beside a Thames barge, the *Pudge* of Rochester, and talked to her skipper and his wife. 'They had been as far as Truro, Gravelines, Hull', just like Mr and Mrs Whittle on the *Welcome* of Rochester:

'She's been foreign many a time,' said Mrs Whittle. 'Gives you quite a turn, coming up out of that companion after a night at sea to find yourself in a foreign harbour and everybody talking Dutch.'

They also met an old fisherman, who explained how eels 'fanged' the worms of a babbing ball 'and said babbing for eels was the most beautiful sport in the whole world'. ('Made like a cowslip ball, said Starboard, and Dorothea was very nearly sick.')

Later that year, Ransome wrote to his mother that he wished he had a plot for his new book. 'It is to be placed on the Broads with all those rivers and hiding places in the dykes, and the little stretches of open water. Really a lovely setting, with herons and bitterns and fish, very wild except just in the holiday months. But, as usual, though I have five youthful characters and one old lady, I haven't the glimmerings of a plot.'

It is interesting that once again the people and the places came first, the plot second. Ransome gathers together a collection of incidents, often ones that he has witnessed or experienced himself, and then thinks out a good framework for them. The letters which he wrote through the years to his friends Margaret and Charles Renold reveal the process by which he worked. He found them very useful advisers and critics. Here is a letter to them which shows how the plot for *Coot Club* began to take shape:

I have masses of things to happen . . . stranding on Breydon . . . voyage in a wherry . . . meeting with a Thames barge . . . shopping at Roy's . . . night with an eel man . . . but main thread still to find. I think one character ought to be concentrated local knowledge so to speak, and he must be my Principal Boy . . . . . aet.12 or 13 . . . living say at Horning. Then I have a pair of twins, girls, who sail with their father in a racing dinghy. They, of course, have somehow to be seduced from their allegiance to Papa in order to take part in the story. Next property is a most spirited old lady, widow, water-colour painter, living in ?boat? er? houseboat? She, I think, impressed by P.B. and perhaps the Twins also, yearns to tune up her great ? nieces? nephews? and therefore gets them down to stay with her for the summer holidays with the object of using the P.B. and the twins to stimulate a livelier spirit than these two well-brought-ups at present possess . . . . There now. What happens? How can I arrange for, say, the Twins to be left behind when the Old Lady and the others sail for Norwich, so that they have the excitement of pursuing without a boat of their own, getting lifts on wherries, tugs, barges, etc.

Do I or do I not bring Dick and Dorothea on from *Winter Holiday*, or is this lot to be an entirely independent world? Independent, I think.

What can be devised by way of triumph, to be achieved by effort and so provide the happy ending that must almost to the end look as if it cannot come off?

You will observe that if all the excitement of the chase right round down to Yarmouth and up the other rivers of the south, to Beccles, Norwich, is given to the Twins . . . it inevitably makes them the chief characters in the book, and tends to cut the ground from under the P.B. and the well-brought-ups, UNLESS some major triumph, Goal, Aim, Achievement can be devised which will be shared by the whole party, and allow the P.B. a chance of coming out strong, so that the chase, etc. while giving the Twins a fine chance of spreading themselves and capturing the reader, will be as it were subservient to the whole . . . or even work as a fuse, delaying, and therefore piling up the interest of the main theme which must for this purpose be already on its way and in the reader's mind.

By reading that letter carefully, and noticing what was used, what was dropped, what was adapted, of those ideas, it is possible to get a good idea of how carefully Ransome thought about his plots which, once written, seem quite effortless. The Goal that he decided on was Bird Protection. The enemy to be routed emerged quite naturally as the ignorant motor-cruising Hullabaloos who had crashed into him as he tacked across Barton Broad. Everything clicked beautifully into place when he realized that Tom Dudgeon's escape from them could be allied to another great cause,

Dick and Dorothea's natural wish to learn to sail after their *Winter Holiday*. With the addition of the Death and Glories as knights errant, saving the day time and again, the plot was complete.

In April 1934 Ransome went to the Broads for another week, checking details and taking photographs to help with the drawings for the book. In Norwich he visited ornithologist Dr Sidney Long, and consulted him about suitable birds. A memorable diary entry reads: 'Suggested water-rail, but said too difficult to see. Better coot or water-hen. Water-hen nests in clumps of trees or rushes. Coots in the water. Plumped for coot.' And so *Coot Club* was born.

In its writing, Port and Starboard receded in importance as characters, as Ransome had foreseen, but their broadland boatshow journey remained an important part of the book. Ransome wrote to the firm that owned *Pudge* of Rochester to ask which bridges she would be likely to use and what cargoes she might carry to Beccles. They replied that she would go round by the New Cut, and would probably carry corn or malt. He always did such homework very thoroughly, asking experts whenever he was in any doubt about his facts.

Another page in his working notebook shows that he had personally experimented with the times of Tom's rowing and sailing of the *Titmouse* up and down the River Bure between Wroxham and Ranworth. His notes often show a daily timetable worked out for the action in the stories – *Coot Club*, with its reliance on tides through Yarmouth, had to be planned minute by minute. He also made lists of the birds which would be right at that time of year, noting what calls they made: 'Bittern booms *until* May. Called "buttles".' They were neatly moved into Dick's notebook; when the children get to Horsey Mere:

Dick covered two pages with "birds seen at Horsey", and began a third . . .

For a long time after lights were out, people were awake in both boats, listening to at least three bitterns booming at each other, and the chattering of the warblers in the reed-beds, the startling honks of the coots, and the plops of diving water-rats.

It was the coots that my own crew on *Glitterwake* noticed first as we glided past the dapper riverside bungalows and thatched boathouses that fringe the river at Wroxham. Plumply hunched, they swam desperately for the bank, or more cunningly *towards* our motorized food trough, with white head flashes signalling vigorously. They showed no signs of dying out. The grebes were shyer. Tilly got out a birdbook, and we identified the exotic-looking great crested grebe's startling head, and found out that the little grebes were also called dabchicks. A flock of Canada geese joined us in Salhouse Broad, confident that we would be cleaning out our larder there. The ducks actually came aboard, waddling round the sidedecks and peering through the windows greedily. It could be people that need protection from birds on the Broads before long. The herons maintained a dignified distance, flapping up towards the Horning heronry.

We were the only boat at Horning staithe (I say this to infuriate people who know what it is like at more crowded times of year) so we could put the *Glitterwake* just where Ransome draws the *Margoletta*, with the Swan Inn in the background. The boatsheds by the New Inn looked very like Jonnatt's (where Pete lost his tooth), even though new houses have been built between them and the staithe. I walked through Horning, little changed from Ransome's description, except for a rash of redwood 'leisure homes' which has destroyed the Wilderness, the Death and Glory's refuge in *The Big Six*. There were still several possible Dudgeon Dykes, and some fine heron weathercocks. The golden bream was an invention of Ransome's own. I had read a little note on Dr Dudgeon's character which made the point that the bream was the defiant gesture of a lone fisherman in a world of sailing fanatics. He was beginning to sound distinctly like Charles Renold, who tried but failed to like sailing Ransome's dinghy *Coch-y-bonddhu*.

Next morning we went on down the River Bure, finding

the Ferry Inn rebuilt and ferryless, and deciding which little dyke on the south bank once held the historic nest No. 7. There was one which looked perfect, but a new duckboard walkway now crosses it more permanently than the *Margoletta* ever did.

'Look! The *Teasel!*' shouted Daisy a little later.

Sure enough, there was a little yacht, moored near Horning Hall where she should have been, awning and all. We waited in vain for William to jump up and bark. William was certainly a real character. He belonged to Charles and Margaret Renold, and even wrote Ransome a letter once,

> Turnfield
> CHeadle
> 7eB. 14th
>
> Dere Mr Ransum
>   1. am ritin to sey thank u for the nice photos of me. an for the gud wishes for mi Birfday. Mi frend Johnny Barlow wud like tu be put in a buke an he ses someone wos staying there who he thort wud put im in a buke an Johnny Barlow is vary vexed cos he ad his face speshully washed + they didnt luke at im.
>   yores trooly
>   Willum Renuld
>
> P.S. Jordan ses thank u for the photo's.

127

puffed up with pride over his forthcoming appearance in *Coot Club*.

That Christmas, Ransome drew the Renolds and William an apologetic Christmas card showing William rampant over a copy of *Coot Club* with the caption: 'Nobody's private life is sacred these days.'

We turned right into Ranworth Dyke and entered Malthouse Broad. It was here, rather than in Ranworth Inner Broad, that Dick and Dorothea had their first sailing lesson in the *Titmouse*. Malthouse Broad is a modern name given to what used to be generally known as Ranworth Broad.

They beat up to the staithe, took the milk-can to the farm, brought it back filled, went to the little shop and post office and sent postcards to Mr and Mrs Callum. One sentence was the same on both cards: 'We have begun to learn to sail.' Then, with a fair wind, they flew back across the Broad to the *Teasel*.

The staithe is no longer its quiet old self. The old malthouses, which burnt down in 1982, have been tastefully rebuilt as a supermarket, the Granary Stores. The pub has been fitted out with a bowsprit in the bar, and much nautical detail, but a little way up the hill the old post office did not seem to have changed since the Callums sent off their proud postcards. In fact, when we asked for cards to send, the owner had to disappear into the back room to find some, puzzled by this early start to the tourist season. A duckboarded Nature Trail led us round the edges of the marshes, through head-high reeds, to Ranworth Inner Broad, where a floating Conservation Centre would have told us all about wildlife if it had been open. Ellen and Susie tried out its drawbridge, which worked by windlass like Tom Dudgeon's.

We motored on, alone on the water as usual, and turned into South Walsham Broad, not much mentioned in the Ransome books, but worth a visit all the same. A pair of cormorants sat on dead trees guarding the entrance to the inner broad, making it seem distant and unreal. It has a wooded island, a thatched boathouse on the shore – the lake in the north in miniature. We moored at the staithe in the outer broad and went in search of milk. It was the first time the crew's legs had been stretched for two days, and a biting east wind turned all ears scarlet. Luckily local savages had hung ropes in some trees, which made swinging across a small stream interesting, while the bo'sun and I continued in search of milk. Farms these days don't seem to expect passing mariners, but a kindly native robbed her own fridge of a bottle for us.

Farther down the River Bure, we passed the ruins of St Benet's Abbey, and then, at last, a sail! It seemed at first to be making good speed across grass, but as we turned up the River Thurne we realized that it was simply several bends of the river ahead of us. It belonged to a slender little racing dinghy, gaff-rigged and half-decked. Like us, she turned into Thurne Dyke, and we rushed on deck to watch as skipper and crew deftly moored, lowered *Tortoiseshell*'s gaff, made her shipshape and headed for the Lion Hotel and lunch. I compared her to the little sketch of *Flash* on the first page of *Coot Club*. She was suspiciously similar. When we went to the Lion for lunch ourselves, her owner told me that she had been built in 1906. I could hardly believe this, but later Robin Richardson, a Potter Heigham boat-builder with a great love for old craft, confirmed that it was true.

'Do you remember that Jim Woodall, the skipper of the wherry in *Coot Club*, asks Port and Starboard about the races? They say *Flash* is out of them, and that they're going to challenge the winner. Jim says he thinks that'll be *Grizzled Skipper*. Now she's a *real* boat – one of the Yare and Bure one-designs. *Tortoiseshell* is another. They were named after butterflies.'

Butterflies? I had thought of *Grizzled Skipper* as an ancient mariner, not a butterfly.

'There are still about a hundred boats of that class in sailing clubs on the Broads,' Robin went on. 'Most of them are wooden, but since the 1950s they've made them of fibreglass. They often race them at Wroxham.'

After a very good lunch at the Lion, which has a play-ground right next door to it, we cruised on up the Thurne to sleepy Womack Water. I had found an old *Handbook to the Broads* in the London Library, and it seemed that this little corner of the world had not changed since 1883, let alone since Ransome's time. 'On the right-hand-side of Womack Water there is a bit of an old-world picture: a boat-builder's shed, large and old, and of picturesque construction under the shade of mighty trees. Beneath it is a wherry, sleepily awaiting repair.' And there it was, wherry and all. Nor was this just any wherry. The *Albion* is now the only wherry left sailing on the Norfolk Broads.

Readers of *Coot Club* will know a little about wherries. The *Sir Garnet* (named after a childhood hero of Ransome's, General Sir Garnet Wolseley) was a working boat, carrying cargoes along waterways that were too weed-tangled for powered craft. Worked by two men, such boats prided themselves on their speed. An express wherry could travel at seven or eight miles an hour. Their single huge sail was used without tanning when it was new, then it was dressed with sea oil and tar, which gave it a rich, dark-brown colour, weathering to black. The mast was mounted on a tabernacle with an enormously heavy counterweight, so that it could be lowered easily at bridges, a manoeuvre a skilled wherryman could carry out so quickly that he would hardly lose speed at all.

There was the bridge, a single span across the river, and with the wind and the tide alike helping her, *Sir Garnet* was sweeping down towards it.

'They'll be too late to get it down,' said Starboard. It did seem impossible that the mast would be lowered before it crashed into the bridge. But Simon and Jim, without a word to each other, seemed not to be hurrying at all. There was a long rattle of the winch paying out the halyard. The huge sail was down. And now, so near the bridge that the twins felt like screaming, the huge mast was dipping towards them, down and down.

130

WHERRIES WAITING FOR THE TIDE AT CANTLEY

'Right O, missie,' said Jim Woodall, and his brown hand closed on the tiller.

'Overslept, eh?' said an old man, looking down from the bridge as the *Sir Garnet* shot through,

'That's with our bein' late on the tide,' said Jim.

And then Jim let them have the tiller again. The mast was lifting the moment they had cleared the bridge. The big black sail rose bellying in the wind. *Sir Garnet* had left Acle Bridge astern of her and was sailing once more.

At one time there were over two hundred wherries trading on the Broads. 'One can hardly imagine the Broads without wherries,' wrote Peter Emerson, a famous Broadland photographer, in 1886. 'They are to be seen at every staithe, as well as in the most sequestered bights, giving no signs of life save that of the galley fire, whose smoke curls lazily upwards.' Specially designed wherry yachts were raced in local regattas, and other wherries were converted during the tourist season into floating hotels, sometimes becoming the Hullabaloos of their age, according to my ancient *Handbook*: 'A wherry fitted up for a yacht was lying near, and her crew had not

131

only got a piano aboard, but played it at seven o'clock in the morning . . . The presence of ladies aboard the wherry, and up so early, was rather a nuisance, as one had to row away for one's dip.'

What ruined the business of the wherries was lorry traffic. The last to be built was the *Ella* of Coltishall in 1912. By 1930 they were 'a dying proposition' and by 1950 there were no trading wherries left at all.

The *Albion* survives because the Norfolk Wherry Trust was formed in 1949 to buy and refit her. Today she looks splendid, fresh from her triumph as the *Sir Garnet* in the recent BBC television film serial of *Coot Club* and *The Big Six* (mysteriously retitled 'Swallows and Amazons for Ever'). She spends her summers taking holiday visitors around the Broads. Her hold sleeps twelve in hammocks hung along its sides, and also houses a kitchen and huge dining table.

'Can I have my birthday party on her?' asked Tilly.

Good idea, I thought, but had to say that it would be too far for us to come for a day. The *Albion*'s skipper, who was touching up her blue and red paint, heard, and to cheer her up asked us all if we would like to have a look inside the small cabin in the stern where he and his mate still sleep on such voyages.

We crowded inside and sat down on the bunks, admiring the little stove, the paraffin lamps on gimbals, and the neat cupboards fitted into every possible corner. It was easy to imagine Port and Starboard sitting where we were, prodding the potatoes and burning the bacon much too crisp for Simon's liking. Then we climbed on to the roof of the hold and looked at the great concrete counterweight, weighing more than a ton, that balanced the mast as it is lowered.

'It's so well balanced that a child of four could see-saw on it,' said the skipper.

Susie looked at it hopefully, and I decided we had better be going.

The day of the wherry may not be over. There are still hulks to be recovered from the muddy dykes. The Norfolk Wherry Trust has raised one, and hopes to collect enough money to refit her as a sister ship to *Albion*. We had seen the skeletal ribs of another beside the Conservation Centre at Ranworth. In the old days, ambitious Norfolk lads used to salvage such hulks, collect ice in them to sell in the fishing ports for a few seasons to make enough money to rig them again, and then start carrying better-paying cargoes. It is possible that holidaymakers could do as much for the survival of wherries as they have for Thames barges, which now carry sailing enthusiasts up and down the East Coast far more often than 'corn to Beccles or malt to London', like *Pudge* of Rochester.

After a night by St Benet's, the ruined abbey interlocked oddly with a windmill, just at the head of South Walsham Broad, and a good place to explore, we turned north up the River Ant, and sailed through Barton Broad to Stalham to get some more provisions. In a boatyard opposite the staithe where we tied up there was an odd bulky boat parcelled in canvas. The children went to have a closer look, and came racing back.

'She's the *Death and Glory*!' shouted Ellen. 'It says so on her side.'

Jane and I left the hot coffee, which was thawing out our fingers after a rather messy attempt at mooring, and followed them. The boat certainly claimed to be *Death and Glory*, and by lifting up the wrapping of canvas I could see a cabin door, though no chimney-pot stove-pipe.

One of the boatyard men came over and explained. It was the boat which had been used in the BBC film.

'It was fine without the cabin, but those poor boys had a terrible job to row her with it on,' he remembered. 'And they couldn't get three bunks into her. They had to film the scenes inside the cabin somewhere else.'

So Ransome's *Death and Glory* must have been rather bigger. More the size of *Kittiwake*, in which he and Evgenia had explored the Baltic.

As well as food for the body, Stalham produced food for thought. In a bookshop ('New and Secondhand, Browsers Welcome') I asked if they had any old books about the

Broads. Tucked away in a cupboard was a real prize. It was a children's adventure story called *The Swan and Her Crew*, written in 1876 by George Christopher Davies. It tells how Frank, Jimmy and Dick build a boat and spend three weeks cruising up and down the Broads, looking at bird and plant

FRONTISPIECE TO G.C. DAVIES, *THE SWAN AND HER CREW*

life, hunting and fishing. In the process it gently informs the reader about Broadland trades and customs. The boys drift out to sea at Yarmouth, and are only saved, after a night of tossing on the turning tide, by some returning fishing boats. They find some poachers' hidden nets, and nearly get caught by them. They eat with gusto: a typical meal consisted of 'first broiled bacon, next tinned salmon, then some gooseberry jam, followed by cheese, and finally a tin of American preserved strawberries, which they had bought in Yarmouth, the whole washed down with coffee and beer'. They take two young hawks from a nest (getting savagely attacked by the parent birds and falling out of the tree in the process) and train them up for hawking. They also watch the passing Broadland craft with interest: wherries, yachts, punts, and the oldest of all, the lateen-rigged keels. Finally, they convert the *Swan* into an ice-yacht in the winter and manage, unlike the Swallows, to 'sail her tolerably close to the wind'.

I felt on reading *The Swan and Her Crew*, a very popular book in its day, that its author must have had some influence on Ransome, not just because of its setting on the Broads, but because of the combination of adventure and information. Like Ransome, G.C. Davies did not let a description of anything technical pass without illustrating it. One page from another of his books, *Wildcat Tower*, 'a story of adventure in the North Country' (Northumberland, not the Lake District), could easily be from a Ransome book. The boys are fishing, and Davies provides two careful drawings of how they knot their lines.

Perhaps Frank, Jimmy and Dick are reborn in the Death and Glories. The *Swan* was as odd a craft as theirs and 'excited any amount of appreciatory and depreciatory comment'. There is also a little incident which marks them out as well qualified to be members of Coot Club. They find a large coot's nest which has broken loose from the bank, and see the old bird swimming around it, and evidently very much puzzled to know what to do.

'Let us tack near her and watch,' said Jimmy. So they sailed round at a distance and watched the poor bird, which followed its boatlike nest as it drifted before the wind. At length the boys were pleased to see the bird make an effort to get on to the nest, and so strongly built was it that it bore her weight well. There she sat, and sailed before the wind at a fair pace.

'Did you ever see the like of that before?'

'No,' answered Frank, 'but I warrant you that the eggs must have been hard set, and near to being hatched, or she would never have done that.'

'She deserves to hatch them, at any rate. Had we better fix the nest or leave it alone?'

'Better leave it alone. I think she will stick it if it does not sink beneath her.'

On Monday evening, the boys sailed about the broad in search of the floating coot's nest, and found it among the reeds at the north end of the broad, and from the broken eggshells in it, they had no doubt but that the coot had hatched her young ones in safety, as she deserved to do.

Far-fetched? Obscure? I would have liked proof that Ransome had read the book. Later on, I found it. A page of his working notebook for *Coot Club* lists some suggestions from Margaret Renold. They were not her best. She thought that the children, hunting the Loch Ness Monster in the Broads on a homemade raft should come on a sunken poacher's bundle attached to the riverbed. Her ideas are rejected, in Ransome's own neat handwriting, as being 'too much like the *Swan*'.

IX

The World's Whopper

Early in *The Big Six*, the Death and Glories take a tow out of trouble by following a fisherman through Potter Heigham, a village farther north on the River Thurne than Womack Water.

The fisherman was watching; and when Joe signalled 'Ready,' headed *Cachalot* for the low, narrow stone arch of the bridge.

'You take her, Joe,' said Pete.

But there was no time to change helmsmen. The *Cachalot* was already nosing in under the arch. The *Death and Glory* followed her.

'Keep her straight,' said Joe. 'She'll clear.'

'Look out for the chimbley,' yelled Pete.

'If the mast clear, that do,' said Bill.

Joe, crouching on the fore-deck and Bill, back in the cockpit, were ready to fend off. They put out their hands and touched the old stones of the arch as they went through.

'Phew!' said Pete with relief when they went out again, and he glanced back over his shoulder. 'It never do look as if there'd be room.'

At the sight of the same narrow, ancient arch, the *Glitterwake* shied nervously to the bank. A curt notice on her dashboard said: THIS CRAFT WILL NOT PASS UNDER POTTER

HEIGHAM BRIDGE. We moored and made for Richardson's, a boatyard well known for its careful restoration of wooden boats. The first thing we saw on the bank was *Madie*, a racing cutter with rapier-sharp lines, her counter stretching away to nothing far behind her rudder. There was a bulb of ballast built into her shallow keel, which allowed her to carry a huge mass of canvas. Ducking in and out of the boatsheds, we found Robin Richardson hard at work on *Buttercup*, built in 1892. He told us that boat-builders designed yachts to race themselves, and then passed them down into their hire fleets. The name *Teasel* might well mean that Ransome meant her as one of this flower-named class.

Such cabin yachts are often Bermuda-rigged today, but there are still some gaff-rigs about. There is no need to know how to sail one before hiring it. The yards give would-be sailors a little instruction, and then they teach themselves as they go. The worst harm they can come to is running aground on the mud. Ransome called it 'the best nursery for sailors there is', and that remains true, although the summer crowds are best avoided.

Across the river, at Herbert Wood's yard, we admired the Lady class yachts with their comfortable cabins, brass trimmings and shapely hulls. The old long bowsprits have disappeared (remember how the Hullabaloos bust someone's bowsprit, and got a hole in old *Margoletta* at the same time, charging across the bows of a sailing-yacht?) and many hire yachts have an auxiliary engine, so quanting can be cut down to a minimum. We asked at Herbert Wood's for a day launch to take us to the upper reaches beyond the bridge. A kindly Scot looked at the four shivering children and the unheated day launch with its summery cane chairs, then at the *Glitterwake*.

'Why don't you take *her* through?' he asked.

'I'd love to,' I said (we had grown quite fond of the pot-bellied old lady by now), 'but she won't go under the bridge.'

'Our pilot'll take her,' he said, pointing to a formidable, oilskin-clad figure, with a weatherbeaten face and a seaman's blue eyes. 'He can get *anything* through.'

Giving way doubtfully but willingly, I called the children out of the yachts they had been investigating, and took them and the pilot aboard. Deftly, he lined up the *Glitterwake*, and twiddling the wheel to and fro nonchalantly shot her under the bridge. Even inside the cabin, I couldn't help ducking. But there we were. I put the pilot off at the staithe and on we went, feeling like early explorers nearing the source of the Nile.

It was here, close to the entrance to Kendal Dyke, that the *Cachalot* had moored while the fisherman went to the Roaring Donkey for milk. We found the narrow dyke which should have led to the Roaring Donkey, although there was no rundown fishing inn at the end of it. I knew that Ransome had moored here himself on a fishing weekend in September 1937, since a note in his diary read: 'Caught nothing of any size. Planned *Cachalot*.' The original *Cachalot* was a whaleship, and her story can be read in Frank T. Bullen's *Cruise of the Cachalot Round the World after Sperm Whales*, which was published in 1898.

We turned up Kendal Dyke, where Dick fell in learning to quant, and had lunch at the entrance to Meadow Dyke, watched by cormorants perched on the great posts that mark the deep channels. Horsey Mere was closed for the sake of the birds. The Norfolk Naturalists' Trust has taken over from the Coot Club, although it was founded a little before they were, in 1926. By restricting entry to the remoter

Broads where birds are nesting, by limiting mooring and powercraft, and by patrolling the waterways, the Trust is making a vital contribution to the preservation of wildlife. The Broads still have their problems. Pollution has meant the disappearance of the water plants and fish which were once so numerous. Holiday crowds inevitably cause serious erosion of the banks. The farmers' interest in efficient drainage confronts the naturalists' high valuation of the marshes. But it could be said that the worst is over. Environmental consciousness is now so high that it is unlikely that what Ransome dreaded, a takeover by Hullabaloos afloat and ashore, will be allowed to happen.

Hickling Broad was open, so we motored on to the north. We had not seen another boat all day, only birds. Instead of Dick's marsh harrier, a smaller hawk (a kestrel, Tilly said) obliged us by hovering over its prey only a few yards from us, and then dropping like a stone to kill. There were so many unfamiliar birds that the bird book was being snatched from hand to hand. Was that a marsh tern or a black-winged grebe? Did Daisy really see a wildly off-course Great Northern Diver, or was she romancing like Dorothea?

We moored at the staithe by the Pleasure Boat Inn, where Ransome noted that 22 lb pike back in 1931. From inside, while tucking into chicken and chips, we saw a lonely windsurfer gathering together his gear and tackle and trim. A wet suit as well as a drysuit, I noticed. He sniffed at the wind and decided to change his sail for a smaller one. He seemed oddly unwilling to start. The bo'sun, who windsurfs when she can't sail, agreed with me that his funboard was quite unsuited to the placid water of the Broad, and that his sail was now too small. Finally he took off, disappointingly ordinary to watch, neither plucky beginner nor spectacular stuntman. We decided that it was probably his first session on the new board he had been given for Christmas, and that what he craved was privacy to try it out. Politely turning our backs, we saw above the door to the main bar a long glass case with an enormous pike grinning glassily out. 'Caught by Mr Herbert-Smith in 1955. 25 lbs.' Bigger than the 22-

pounder that Ransome had seen, but still not 'the World's Whopper'.

The barman turned out to know all about pike.

'Thirty pounds? Easily. Someone caught a forty-pounder in 1967. And in 1971, a local chap returned a forty-five pounder.'

'Returned?'

'Put it back.'

'Then how did he know how much it weighed?'

'Oh, he's a very truthful man,' the barman assured me, looking me straight in the eye, arms stretched out to show the size of the whopper.

I looked out of the window at the windsurfer and back at the twenty-five pounder. It was quite big enough.

Ransome's books are well known to have taught many children to sail so well that they have been able to handle a boat as soon as they stepped into one. It is less often pointed out that they are full of excellent advice on fishing. Tickling trout in *The Picts and the Martyrs*, fly-fishing on Trout Tarn in *Swallowdale*, catching perch in Shark Bay, setting nightlines for eels in *Secret Water*, and, most spectacularly, pike-fishing in *The Big Six*, are all accurately described. Fishermen who want to improve on techniques learnt from these books can try Ransome's two books on fishing, *Rod and Line*, and *Mainly about Fishing*. They are not entirely about fishing. Readers eager for more Ransome will find much to enjoy in them.

We motored across the Broad, trying to give the wind-surfer the fun of a few waves, and came back to Potter Heigham. Our pilot was busy managing the slings that were swinging a pretty little sailing yacht from the sheds into the water. Some lucky person was taking her out in a day or two for some peaceful, if chilly, sailing. The pilot told me about the October races when the boatyard men take out all the sailing boats and race them. Broads yachts have been racing since the beginning of the nineteenth century. The oldest of the clubs, the Royal Norfolk and Suffolk, was founded in 1859, and held regattas at Wroxham, Oulton and Cantley. In those days most of the racers were cutters and lateen-rigged yachts. As racing became more sophisticated, yachts were made with flat floors, fin keels, balanced rudders. 'Mountains of canvas supported by molehills of yachts' was Davies's description of the scene at Wroxham regatta in 1882, the same 'far-off days' which were in the mind of the Admiral, 'when Breydon Water was gay with yachts, and she was listening for the crack of the winning gun in the commodore's steam launch'. The Horning Sailing Club, to which Mr Farland and Port and Starboard must have belonged, was started in 1909.

A couple of days later, we met the Herbert Wood's yacht, *Fine Lady*, on a narrow part of the River Ant. I threw the engine into reverse and veered into the bank so that we could stop and admire her. All hands came on deck to cheer, and *Fine Lady*'s crew acknowledged us very kindly, admitting to frozen fingers and some envy of *Glitterwake's* central heating. We, on the other hand, longed to be aboard such a *Teasel* lookalike. Apart from her Bermuda rig, she was just the sort of boat that Ransome and his friends hired for the adventures of the Northern River Pirates later on in the 1930s.

In 1938, 'a perfect fleet' sailed from Wroxham in four Fairways and two Whippets. Ransome and Evgenia sailed the flagship naturally, a Fairway. Three families whom they had met at Pin Mill were in the other Fairways, the Youngs, the Arnold-Forsters, and George Russell and his cousin Raymond Hubbard. The Youngs, a large family with four sons, also had one of the Whippets, which their eldest three sons sailed alone. Those boys now run the family firm, Young's Brewery at Wandsworth, where the drays are still pulled by shire-horses. The crew of the last Whippet were a fine surprise. Two lakeland pirates had crept into this real Broadland adventure, though they were kept out of the storybook ones. It was sailed by Taqui and Titty Altounyan.

All Northern River Pirates flew Jolly Roger flags; the Youngs still have theirs, a particularly striking one, with large teeth which 'rose and fell like clappers' when the flag rippled in the wind. George Russell kept a log of the voyage, which his sister Josephine lent me to read. It is a unique document, written in pencil that is now very faded, in a small black notebook bought from Roy's in Wroxham. In it I read about 'Barnacle Bill' and his 'whistle-blowing mate' Evgenia in action: streaking away from the fleet while less lark-like crews were still tussling with their toothpaste, dispensing grog to all hands, and leading late-night sing-songs after feasting on Christmas pudding laced with the medicinal rum. No doubt it was an improvement on the Death and Glories' methylated spirit. Here are a few highlights from the log.

> We sailed on past the black sheep till we caught sight of Titty and Taqui involved with a large enemy. Further on we saw another pirate at grips with five large boats, so we entered the fray sneaking up under the big boat's stern when she was in irons and approaching Horning in Titty and Taqui's wake. We were very nearly rammed by a beastly wherry yacht just below the Swan, and we docked successfully under Barnacle Bill's eagle eye . . .
>
> We settled down to a quiet lunch and snooze, never realizing that Roger [the youngest Young] had fallen in without his jacket on and had been rescued fully clothed by Titty. Famous last words: 'I could not help it. Where is my choc-bar?' . . .
>
> We tacked and tacked and quanted and quanted till we came in sight of Wroxham, and in the excitement of crying 'Land! Land!' and smacking our parched lips we were nearly rammed by a convoy of Hullabaloos towed by a motor launch.

The following year Josephine Russell crewed for her brother George. The Youngs and the Arnold-Forsters signed on again, but the Altounyans were busy elsewhere. Instead, two keen sailors of ten and eight, Vicky and Susan Reynolds, joined the fleet with their parents. Vicky, now Mrs McNair, told me that the highlight of the voyage for her was the primus stove in their cabin catching fire (fortunately it was soon put out). She remembered evenings spent in the

Ransomes' cabin, listening to him telling old African folk tales about 'a strange spider called Anansi'. One of Josephine Russell's snapshots of the cruise shows Vicky, Susan and Ransome at Thurne Dyke, leaning back into the '90 mile an hour gale!' logged by George on April 17th. The experienced sailors of the second cruise showed a bloodthirsty confidence:

> After we got into the Bure we met a whole lot of boats going the same way and the circus began. James [Young] and our boat dealt with five of them so effectively that they were forced to tie up at the side. One of them rammed us, and was so forcibly pushed off by the mate that they promptly went into the bank . . . The mate sailed her about in Wroxham Broad for half an hour . . . until we saw the Ransomes and the Youngs coming in at the other end. We sailed to meet them, took photographs and went on up the river and then the bloody battle began. We layed alongside, soaked the other pirates, were soaked ourselves, but captured their mop, which we duly hoisted to the masthead. LONG LIVE THE NORTHERN RIVER PIRATES

After all this real-life action, perhaps it was right that *The Big Six* should have become a story of united action against an enemy, although there is no light-hearted pirate fantasy about it. The Death and Glories have become more sober, a Salvage Company, and the framework of the book is that of a detective story.

> 'But who are the Big Six?' asked Pete.
> 'It's the Big Five really,' said Dorothea. 'They are the greatest detectives in the world. They sit in their cubby-holes in Scotland Yard and solve one mystery after another.'
> 'But why Six?'
> 'There are only five of them and there are six of us,' said Dorothea.

The idea of a detective story came from Margaret Renold. Perhaps she had read C.P. Snow's first published novel,

Death under Sail, which also mentions the Big Five, and tells of a murder on a wherry-yacht sailing from Wroxham to Horning. We can see the way Ransome's mind was working in this letter to her in January 1938:

> Detective. Why not? Now then. George Owden of Coot Club is obviously the right criminal. Tom and the Death and Glories are the right detectives, with the help of Dorothea's imagination and Dick's scientific mind. Now, I see it this way. It would be all wrong for the detectives to snoop out of public spirit with the hope of handing George over to justice. The detective work must be forced upon them to clear themselves of some villainy of which, thanks to George Owdon, they are bearing the blame. What the devil can it be? What can George have done and done in such a way that everybody thinks the Death and Glories are responsible?
>
> Come on, Margaret . . . Something that can be placed on the Broads, and timed for October or November, or even for the week before Christmas. This because I have a very gorgeous episode with a pike, and a fisherman, and an inn-keeper and the Death and Glories, which it would be a waste not to work in. And because I want to get a cold weather story if possible, because of being able to get some fun out of the cabin those three have built in their old boat, with an old coal stove and a genuine chimney pot on the cabin roof. (There is a ghastly episode when they try to smoke eels in the cabin, and a fine one where they have a Christmas pudding and use a lot of methylated to get the flames, and subsequently a lot of sugar in the hope of taking the taste away). I've got a lot of good stuff simmering about the Death and Glories and would just love to do you a good detective story about them if you can go a bit further in devising the crime to make it possible. (After *Coot Club* it must have nothing to do with visitors' boats.)

Of course, in the end, that was exactly what the plot *was* about. Was it Margaret's idea? Or did she just think of it because Ransome said it was out of the question? We don't

AN ILLUSTRATION FROM E. SUFFLING, *HOW TO ORGANIZE A HOLIDAY ON THE BROADS*: DID IT INSPIRE THE LINE BETWEEN *TITMOUSE* AND *TEASEL*?

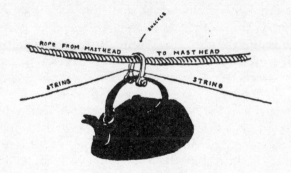

know. He often referred to *The Big Six* as 'your book' in letters to her, and it was certainly dedicated 'To Margaret and Charles Renold'.

By the time *Glitterwake* wallowed back to Wroxham at the end of our lonely week on the Broads, Tilly and Daisy could steer as well as I could, and were raring to be let loose in a cabin yacht, like Titty and Taqui. We still had the southern rivers to explore; next October perhaps, in *Daffodil*, or one of the Lady class. As we came round the big bend just after Wroxham Broad, we saw a small fishing dinghy in midstream. The two boys in it were both standing up, and made no attempt to get out of our way. One was hanging on to his arching rod like grim death, the other was holding a landing net at the ready. Suddenly out of the water came a great gleaming monster, twisting viciously. A pike. Not the world's whopper, but quite a shark all the same.

One thing had been handsomely proved by *The Cruise of the Glitterwake Round the Broads in Search of Ransome*: there is still plenty there for sailors, fishermen and pirates to enjoy.

TOM DUDGEON WITH THE PUG WILLIAM — AN UNUSED
RANSOME SKETCH

X
Peter Duck Spins His Yarn

There is a puzzling contradiction for the Ransome reader who happens to come to *Peter Duck* before *Swallowdale*. Did the children really sail in *Wild Cat* to Crab Island, and outwit Black Jake helped by Peter Duck, who then returned home to Norfolk to share his time between his three daughters at Potter Heigham, Beccles and Acle? Or was the ancient mariner invented on a winter holiday on the Broads, to be a useful imaginary companion for Titty on future occasions? 'Their Own Story', the first two chapters of an early draft for *Peter Duck*, explains the mystery. Despite its unfinished quality, it is interesting to read for two reasons. Firstly, it shows how completely differently the story of *Peter Duck* might have been handled. Secondly, it describes the Norfolk winter holiday on a wherry, which is referred to at the beginning of *Swallowdale*, and so gives us a quite new instalment of the adventures of Captain Flint, the Swallows and the Amazons. It is also interesting that the monkey, Gibber, was originally called Jacko. Ransome started to change Jacko to Gibber in 'Their Own Story', but did not do so all the way through. Jacko is the name of E.F. Knight's pet monkey in *The Cruise of the Falcon*.

Their Own Story
by Arthur Ransome

'The light's burning all right but the fog's as thick as ever,'

said Titty, shutting the door of the cabin at the foot of the
companion way quickly behind her, but not quickly enough
to stop a cold breath from outside and a soft cloud of fog
from slipping through into the warm lamplight of the cabin.
It was a big wide cabin, as big as the main cabin of the
houseboat on the lake where they had banqueted on the day
of the battle as soon as Captain Flint had got into some dry
clothes after walking the plank. They were all there, the four
Walkers, Captain John, Mate Susan, Able-seaman Titty and
the Ship's Boy, Roger, who had sailed the *Swallow* during
that adventure of the summer, and the Blacketts, Captain
Nancy and her Mate Peggy, who had sailed the *Amazon*. It
was just two days after Christmas. Captain Flint's book (that
was found on Cormorant Island) had been a great success and
Captain Flint, instead of going away for the winter, as he had
planned, had stayed in England instead. He had hired a
wherry, which is a very big sort of boat with one great sail,
on the Norfolk Broads and had invited the Blacketts, who
were his nieces, and the Walkers, but for whom he would
have lost his book, to come and spend part of the Christmas
holidays with him.

A wherry is a good big boat. This one had four good
sleeping cabins in her, besides the saloon, and the galley, and
the fo'c'sle. Captain Flint, whose real name was Turner, slept
in the fo'c'sle. Captain John, home from school, shared a
cabin with the Boy Roger, just as he had shared a tent on the
island. Mate Susan and Able-seaman Titty shared a cabin.
Captain Nancy and Mate Peggy shared a cabin. The fourth
cabin was occupied at night by Roger's monkey, given him
by Captain Flint soon after the adventures of the summer.
The parrot slept in his cage in the saloon, but it would not
have been safe to leave the monkey and the parrot together.

Just now they were all in the main saloon, waiting for
Captain Flint to come back from the village near by. The
wherry, the *Polly Ann*, was moored to the bank. A plank had
been laid across as a gangway, and a lantern had been hoisted
in the rigging to help Captain Flint to find his way back to
the ship. The able-seaman had been sent up to see if it was

burning. When she came back she found the others talking about a book called *Swallows and Amazons*.

'It must be written by someone who knows us,' said Mate Susan. 'You can tell that because he's got such a lot of the things that happened right.'

'But just look at the things he's got wrong,' said Mate Peggy.

'I don't see how anybody could know what we felt,' said Titty, 'and he's always pretending he knew.'

'We're all a bit different from what we really are,' said Captain John. 'Just look how tidy he's made Susan.'

'Well she is tidy,' said Roger.

'Tidier than you,' said John, 'but not as tidy as all that.'

'Daddy said he thought Captain Flint wrote it,' said Susan. 'Mother sent a copy out to him in Hong Kong, and when he wrote back to say thank you he asked her to send his compliments to Captain Flint and to say that he did not mind having his telegram printed, but that if half the things in the book were true he thought we all deserved to be drowned several times over, duffers or not duffers. It was the sailing at night that upset him.'

John opened his mouth to say something, but shut it again.

'I don't believe Captain Flint wrote it,' said Nancy. 'If he had it would have been much better. He's been all over the world so he wouldn't have put down only the things that happened to us. That book makes out it's a story but you've only got to read it to see that it's just telling the truth, or trying to anyhow. No it's just someone has pieced together the things we did and put them in the book. Why, even their map is a copy of ours and misses out lots of the places that we know of. Anyhow, if it was Uncle Jim telling a story he'd tell one worth hearing, with all sorts of things happening that couldn't happen on the lake at home. He always made things hum when he was with us there, but if he were making up a story and letting himself go, it would be something a lot better than *Swallows and Amazons*.'

'Let's make him tell one,' said Titty.

'Shiver my timbers,' said Nancy Blackett, 'why shouldn't we all tell it. He won't be able to think of everything that ought to happen.'

'It would be much better than having anything read aloud,' said Peggy.

'We could alter it as we went along,' said Titty. 'Supposing we didn't like what was happening.'

'Who would be in it?' asked Peggy.

'All of us, of course,' said Nancy.

'And Polly?' said Titty.

'And Gibber?' asked Roger.

'Both of them,' said Captain Nancy, 'and of course we could put in lots of other people, you know, for walking the plank, or being drowned, or eaten by sharks or anything like that.'

'That's much the best way in a story,' said Titty. 'Something always goes wrong, and it's much better for it to go wrong with the people you don't really like.'

'But if we all make it up, who will tell it?' asked Susan. 'I can't, and Roger is too young, and John can't and Titty would get much too excited.'

'Peggy would chatter on so much that nothing would ever happen,' said Nancy. 'And I don't mind doing things but I can't tell about them. Captain Flint'll have to do the telling, and we'll stop him if he goes wrong. He'll tell it quite well, and anyhow we can make sure it's good by telling him what to put in.'

*

'*Polly Ann* ahoy!' There was a loud shout on the bank outside.

Titty was nearest the door, because she had come in from seeing that the lantern was all right, and so she was first out and hurrying up the companion ladder to the dripping, slithery deck.

'Ahoy!' she shouted as loud as she could.

'Ahoy there!' shouted Nancy, who had run up after her.

'Ahoy!' shouted John.

'Ahoy!' shouted Roger.

Peggy and Susan, the two mates, as soon as they heard the first shout had jumped up and run into the cooking galley, to turn up the oil stove and bring the kettle to the boil. It was already hot. Susan warmed up the teapot by making the steam from the spout of the kettle go into it. Peggy slapped out seven tin plates and seven mugs on the cabin table. Between them they had things ready for tea in only about three minutes more than no time.

At Christmas time on the Broads it is dark soon after four o'clock, and now it was getting on for half past five. Captain Flint had been a long time buying all the things that were needed, and for once he had not wanted to take any of the others with him, because of the deep mud. He had said that he would find it quite enough to look after one pair of feet, coming along the dyke in the dark.

The four on deck could see a light moving across the marshes. It came nearer and nearer. John took out his pocket torch and waved it in circles. The light on land swung rapidly from side to side and then up and down to show that Captain Flint had seen the signal. He could see where the *Polly Ann* was because of the light in her rigging, but, after all, there might have been other vessels moored to the bank about there. The river winds to and fro, and nothing is easier than to make for the wrong light.

A few minutes later Captain Flint, a huge knapsack on his back, a lantern in one hand and an enormous loaf of bread in the other, appeared on the bank in the light of his own lantern and walked carefully across the plank gangway to the deck.

'I'll be having your mothers fighting each other for which is to murder me first,' he said, 'if you get your deaths of colds coming on deck without coats. First rule in the *Polly Ann* this voyage. No one takes a spell on deck without dressing for it.'

He was just the same fat, baldheaded man he had been in the summer. But now, instead of a sunhat he wore a sou'wester, and though it was not raining his oilskins were shining wet with little drops of water all over them, making the black oilskins look grey in the light of the lantern.

'It's not freezing,' he said, 'but it's precious near it and it's going to freeze tonight. We'll take the drawbridge aboard. I shan't be going ashore again and no one is likely to come calling on us.'

They pulled the plank aboard and stowed it out of the way along the top of the cabin roof, where the handrail at the side kept it from falling off. Then they hurried down into the warm steaming cabin, and Captain Flint was just going to empty his knapsack of provisions on the table, when Mate Susan stopped him.

'Peggy's laid it for tea,' she said. 'And tea's ready.'

'Aye, aye, Mister Mate,' said Captain Flint, 'but there's two dozen doughnuts that'll be better on the tea-table than in that knapsack. You fish them out, Peggy. The rest of the stuff is just stores, mates' business, for you and Susan to deal with later on.'

A few minutes later they were all sitting behind their steaming mugs. Tea on the *Polly Ann* was a real tea. As Nancy Blackett said, 'There was no nibbling about it.' You sat down to the cabin table and ate what you thought would last you until next day's breakfast. It never quite did. You were ready for a bowl of hot bread and milk to finish off the day with a few hours later. But tea, while it lasted, was a serious affair, and there was not much talking until the cold turkey and the fried plum pudding and the bread and butter was all done and everybody had had a second mug of tea, and they were all eating their way through their last doughnuts.

Then Captain Nancy brought them back to what they had been talking about when they had heard Captain Flint's call from the land.

'We were talking about *Swallows and Amazons*,' she said. 'Look here, Uncle Jim, Captain Flint, I mean, did you write it or didn't you?'

'Of course I didn't,' said Captain Flint.

'Honest Pirate you didn't?'

'Honest Pirate.'

'We thought you hadn't. If you had, you'd have done it much better. You see, really that book only tries to tell just what happened. What's the good of that? It happened anyway, whether anyone tells about it or not. And it's silly being tied down like that. Why shouldn't we have a properly gorgeous story, much better than anything that could have happened to us on the lake with little boats like *Swallow* and *Amazon*.'

'*Swallow*'s a good little ship,' said John.

'Who said she wasn't?' said Nancy. 'It's her size. You called her "little" yourself. Now if we made the story ourselves, we could have a really big ship, big enough to go anywhere.'

'We could sail round the world,' said Titty.

'We could make a story that would be some fun for us instead of just for other people,' said Nancy.

'I'd like a schooner better than any other kind of ship,' said John. 'There was one in Falmouth harbour once that really had sailed round the world.'

'But in a story we could have a liner,' said Peggy, 'with a cabin each all round, and one for Gibber and one for Polly and still with a lot to spare for friends we might happen to meet.'

'Four decks,' said Susan. 'We shouldn't need all of them, so we could put plenty of earth on one of them, and sow it with grass, and keep a cow or two, so that we shouldn't have to drink that horrible condensed milk they give you in ships. Or perhaps goats would be better. Surer-footed. Even liners roll a bit sometimes.'

'We'd have lots of hens too,' said Peggy. 'Fresh eggs every day.'

'It's kind of the mates to think so much of our meals,' said Captain Flint, 'but, you know, I don't think we could manage a liner. There'd be the engines.'

'I'll run the engines,' said Roger.

'You won't see much if you're down with the engines all the time,' said John. 'I'm not going to help you with them. Far better stick to sail.'

154

'What about a full-rigged ship?' said Titty. 'A real beauty, like the *Cutty Sark* in the picture.'

'Wants a big crew to handle her properly,' said Captain Flint. 'Fore and aft's the thing. I'm all for a schooner, or a ketch. And there's nothing against having an auxiliary motor in her, so that we shouldn't be held up by calms. Roger could be chief engineer and he could teach Jacko to go round with the oil-can. A ketch is easiest to handle. But the seven of us could sail a schooner easily.'

'Let's have a schooner,' said Titty, 'like the one in *Treasure Island*.'

'How many cabins?' asked Susan.

'I don't see why we shouldn't have one each,' said Captain Flint, 'if the Mates can do without too much livestock and we don't need to leave too much room for the pearls and the gold and all the rest of it that we shall pick up on the voyage.'

'Low and rakish,' said Nancy, 'the fastest that ever sailed.'

'What's her name?' asked Titty.

There was a pause.

'We'll think of that when we get her started. We'll paint it on before we leave the channel,' said Nancy.

'When do we start?' asked Captain Flint.

'Why shouldn't we have started already?' said Captain Nancy.

'Why not?' said Captain Flint. 'But how are you going to tell the story?'

'You're going to tell it,' said Nancy Blackett, 'only it won't be interrupting if anyone has a good bit to put in.'

'I hope it'll all be good bits,' said Captain Flint. 'Then I shall be able to listen instead of telling.'

'We'll all listen and we'll all tell it,' said Nancy. 'Nobody can remember everything. Anyhow, don't let's waste time. We've started.'

'What time of year is it?' asked Captain Flint.

'The opposite from this,' said Nancy. 'Now you see why it's going to be so much better than *Swallows and Amazons*. The man who wrote that book would be telling the truth and saying it was dark at half past four and frosty outside and a fog and us tied up to the bank in a wherry. Not that the wherry isn't very nice. But now we're in a schooner, and it's early summer. May, for example.'

'All right,' said Captain Flint. 'May. And we've sailed out of Lowestoft harbour and past the Sunk Lightship and the Galloper and the North Goodwin. We saw the revolving light on the North Foreland before the watch below turned in, and now it's a grand May morning, bright sunshine, and the schooner is running down the channel before a fresh north easter, smooth water, with the wind off the land,'

'Bringing a smell of lilac,' said Titty. 'And you ought to say the schooner had a bone in her teeth, with the white ripple at her bows.'

'She has,' said Captain Flint. 'Captain John is steering, and the two mates are towing the breakfast things astern, fastened up in a basket so that the sea will do their washing up for them.'

'Tin plates, of course,' said Susan.

'Titty and Polly are up in the bows, enjoying the sunshine. Captain Nancy is looking at the chart and ticking off the light-houses as we bring them abeam. I'm lying on deck in the lee of the deckhouse, smoking a pipe.'

'And Jacko?' asked Roger. 'He'd like to be out if it's a really hot day.'

'Jacko's up at the masthead, keeping a good look out. And as for Roger, he isn't looking after the engine, because we've got a good wind. No. He's hanging over the bows, sitting in a bosun's chair, with a pot of paint beside him, painting in the name of the ship, like Nancy said.'

'But what is the name?' said Roger. 'I can't paint it in if I don't know it.'

'There's something in that,' said Captain Flint. 'Has anybody got a good name?'

No one answered.

'Don't let's be in too much of a hurry,' said Captain Flint. 'We must have a really good name for the schooner. We'll sleep on it. Someone'll think of a good one. Meanwhile Roger's sitting there, outside the bows, with the blue water and the white foam beneath him as the schooner swings along down channel, and he's filled his brush with paint and is just going to begin painting in the first letter of the name. As soon as anybody knows what it is we'll let him paint it in. And now, what about getting the washing up over? It's not much good trailing a basket of plates astern of the *Polly Ann* while she's tied up to the bank. And then for hot bread and milk to keep the cold out, and then for bed. In the morning we'll know the name of our schooner, and we'll know why we're hurrying down the channel and what Jacko is looking for from the masthead.'

'It's a pity he doesn't know it's summer,' said Roger, as, later on, he said goodnight to the little monkey snuggled up in its blankets.

When all the Walkers and Blacketts were in their bunks and long after all was quiet in the wherry, Titty heard Captain Flint tapping out his pipe in the cabin. 'I wonder if he's got the name,' she said to herself, and went on thinking of name after name. She thought of the names of all the ships she had ever seen, and with each name she saw the ship, a long procession sailing past, ship after ship, too many to count, and many still to come when at last she fell asleep.

Chapter II

Next morning there was another cold raw fog lying low over the fens. From only a dozen yards away on the dyke nothing of the *Polly Ann* could be seen but the top of her mast and the upper parts of her shrouds and her forestay, from which the lantern was hanging, glittering feebly in the clear air above the mist. But anyone would have known there were people in her. There were the noises of getting up going on in three cabins at once, and the noise of Captain Flint swilling down the decks with water dipped from the river while he sang 'Oh, it's up in the morning early', not more than a verse of it at a time, because he had to stop to thump himself about the chest to keep his hands from freezing. Down below in the main cabin things were warm enough, for he had a good fire going in the stove, and kettles boiling on the oil cookers, and a big double saucepan of oatmeal porridge simmering on the top of the stove.

The gangway plank was laid between the wherry and the shore, and presently old Peter Duck came out of the fog and stepped carefully aboard with a big can full of milk from a farm near by, where the farmer's wife was a niece of his.

It was already their second day on the wherry, and the Walkers and Blacketts were not in such a hurry to be up and about as they had been on the lake in the summer. With this fog it was dark all day in the little cabins, and even in the big saloon they kept a lantern burning. Also it did not get light until fairly late. Still, a few minutes after Peter Duck came back with the milk, Susan was busy with the teapot and Peggy was ladling out porridge into bowls, the able-seaman was laying the table, and the ship's boy was banging on the ship's bell, to show that breakfast was ready.

'Anybody got a name for our schooner?' asked Captain Flint. 'Roger's arm'll be getting stiff, holding the paintbrush ready to paint in the first letter of her name.'

Everybody waited for everybody else. Nobody spoke for a minute. Then old Peter Duck spoke. 'I was looking at that book you was talking about, not to read it, of course, but seeing there was a chart in it, and I found the plan of an island there. Good name that island's got. Wild Cat. It'd be a good name for a schooner I was thinking.'

'Well done, Peter,' said Nancy Blackett. 'Why shouldn't we call the schooner after the island?'

'It's the best island in the world,' said Titty.

'And it's a very good name,' said John.

'Anyone got a better name?' said Captain Flint. There was no answer. 'Right,' he said, 'then Roger can let fly with his paintbrush. The schooner *Wild Cat* is bowling down channel in the summer sunshine, with a north easter off the land, a bone in her mouth, and Roger sitting in a bosun's chair slung over the starboard bow painting in the letters. He's got as far as the W already.'

'I've got farther than that,' said Roger.

'Get ahead with it then,' said Nancy, 'and then we'll sling you over the port bow to paint the name on that side. After that, there'll be the stern.'

'There'll be the port to paint in there,' said John, 'as well as the name. *Wild Cat. Lowestoft.*'

'I know why we're in a hurry,' said Titty. 'It's got to do with Mr Duck.'

'Well, you talk it over with him before you tell us,' said Captain Flint. 'We want to shift the *Polly Ann* today, about ten miles up river, and by the time we've done that, Roger will have finished with the paintwork on the schooner and we can get on with the story.'

'What about the fog?' asked John.

'Fog'll lift before noon,' said Peter Duck, 'and there'll be a bit of an easterly wind. You can feel it coming, bringing the cold on its back.'

'Mr Duck says there may be a hard frost coming, when we shan't be able to move, so I want to get the *Polly Ann* to some place where it's not quite so far to bring the milk and get food. And there's letters from home to think of. There's a post office in the village up river. I want to move there while we can.'

'Ice?' cried Nancy. 'Will the *Polly Ann* be frozen in?'

'Likely enough,' said Peter Duck. 'She's been frozen in before, but it isn't often anyone rents her this time of year.'

'We'll shift her to a better place, so that we'll be all right whether she freezes in or not,' said Captain Flint.

'It'll be like being frozen in in the Arctic,' said Titty. 'Only no polar bears. We shall go on the ice and then in the evenings we'll sit in the cabin and go on with the voyage of the *Wild Cat*.'

'That's the way to look at it,' said Captain Flint. 'The more the wherry sticks in one place, the further we can go in the schooner.'

'Hurry up now,' said Captain Nancy, 'and let's shift the wherry while we can.'

*

The ropes were stiff and white with hoar frost, and Captain Flint and Peter Duck between them had a hard time in hoisting the wherry's great sail, even with the other two captains, Nancy and John, hanging on to ropes where they could and making the most of their weight. The Walkers and Blacketts all wore their woolly jerseys, like Captain Flint and Peter Duck, and over their jerseys they had short warm coats, and mufflers round their necks and thick woollen gloves. They were warm enough, and Captain Flint kept them busy. Roger brought Jacko to the companion way, cuddled up inside his coat, so that nothing but his head showed. But it was too cold on deck for monkeys, so Jacko was left below in the warmth.

'Never mind,' said Roger as he left him, 'you're going to have a fine time in the story. It's summer and schooners have two masts, almost a forest for you.'

The fog lifted with the easterly wind, and the sun shone out. They cast off from the bank and began to move up river, between the sparkling frosted sedges at the river sides.

As the *Polly Ann* moved up the river, the wake she left astern of her sent its ripples to the sedges, and all the way up the river there was a long tinkling as the ripple broke the cat ice among the reeds.

Far away beyond the reeds they saw windmills and sometimes a haystack or an old church, but very few trees. At one place they saw the heads of people moving this way and that too fast to be walking. When they stood on the cabin roof, they could see that the people were skating on the frozen marsh.

'If it keeps on like this, the river'll close up, sure enough. It'll close sudden,' said Peter Duck.

It was very cold and nobody was sorry to take a turn below in the warmth of the big cabin. Jacko was shut up in his box in his private stateroom, but the door was left open for the heat to come in from the stove. He was kept there

Houseboat something like this

408 THE "GONDOLA" ON CONISTON LAKE
(ABRAHAMS' SERIES)

21-2 The *Gondola* (*above*) as Ransome marked her up for Clifford Webb's drawing of Captain Flint's houseboat, and (*below*) sailing once again as a passenger steamer on Coniston Water. Wetherlam (High Topps) is in the background.

23-7 Ransome's own boats: *Slug* (*top left*) was his first command, but Evgenia could make *Kittiwake* (*top right*) more homely. *Racundra* (*centre left*), the first boat he designed, crewed here by the real Peter Duck. Ransome called the *Nancy Blackett* (*centre right*) 'the best little boat I ever had' and his ketch *Peter Duck* (*left*) 'a sort of marine bath-chair for my old age'.

28-30 The 'hollywoods': Dick and Desmond Kelsall and Peggy and Joan Hudson pose for the *Peter Duck* drawings, 'Hard at Work' (*above*), 'Sums' (*right*) and a capstan-turning tailpiece (*below*).

31-3 The Northern River pirates: (*top*) Ransome's fleet moored on the Norfolk Broads; (*centre*) Ransome and the Reynolds girls at Thurne Dyke; (*below*) Evgenia, the whistle-blowing mate, checks her stores.

because it was safer to leave Polly in charge of the cabin by herself. Peggy and Susan cooked a huge dish of hot bacon and eggs for the middle of the day, and wanted to tie up to the bank so that everybody could come down and have dinner together. But the wind was not strong and the wherry was moving very slowly, and Captain Flint and Peter Duck didn't want to waste a minute. So while Captain Flint had his food, Captain Nancy stayed on deck with Peter Duck, in case anything was wanted, and when Peter Duck came down for his turn, Captain Flint and Captain John took charge on deck. It's tricky work steering a big wherry, even with the wind free and light, and not even Captain Nancy felt quite like taking the tiller by herself. Captain Flint didn't like to talk while he was steering. Peter Duck, of course, was used to it and didn't mind talking at all. He and Titty had a good deal to say to each other. Once, when Captain Flint was coming to take the tiller, he heard the old man say, 'That's right. There's some in Lowestoft that wouldn't stick at nothing.'

'What's that?' said Captain Flint. 'What's that about Lowestoft?'

'You'll know later on,' said Titty. 'I was just making sure that I did know why we were in such a hurry in the schooner.'

'I can think of one good reason,' said Captain Flint. 'It was to keep in the sunlight as long as you could by sailing west.'

'You'd have to go about and sail east after sunset if you was to do that, wouldn't you Cap'n,' said Mr Duck.

'You're right, Mr Duck,' said Captain Flint. 'West by day and east by night, backwards and forwards, meeting the sun and then running after it. I wonder no one's ever thought of it before.'

Titty looked hard at Captain Flint and then at Mr Duck.

'We weren't sailing backwards and forwards in the schooner,' she said. 'We were sailing west as hard as we could go, with topsails set. We were in such a hurry that if we'd had a poop we'd have set the little boat sail on it, like Columbus did.'

161

XI

Wild Cat

Arthur Ransome wrote those pages of 'Their Own Story' straight after finishing *Swallows and Amazons*. The idea for it probably came from his request to the Altounyan children in Syria for more ideas for adventures. Here is part of Titty's reply:

> As you asked for some subjects for your new book I will try to think of some. Make it with treasure or something hidden somewhere – on an island of course so there will be something about boats in it – and let the Swallows (that is, if you are going to write about them again) find it after a *lot* of adventures. And let everyone make a discovery of some sort. Of course, this is a very bad idea, and perhaps Taqui or Susie will give better ones, but that's the only idea I have.

The two older girls also suggested desert islands and treasure hunts, and added wild boar hunts and camping in nests in trees. Taqui was keen on 'Swallows in Syria', and three pages of a rough draft for it by Ransome survive. The different voices adding to and improving upon each others' ideas make a good start to the Peter Duck story, but it would have been tedious to have had to keep on digressing from the tale to everyday life on the wherry (riveting as those details are to the Ransome-hungry). Because 'Their Own Story' wasn't working, Ransome gave it up, and concentrated on *Swallow-*

dale. The reference to Peter Duck in Chapter IV of that book – 'Titty had had a big share in his invention' – makes it clear that he was determined to go back to him, and early in 1932 he did.

The new version was planned on board the steamer which took Ransome and Evgenia most of the way to Syria to visit the Altounyan family in Aleppo, bringing them a dinghy to sail at Antioch. Ransome took careful notes from the *Channel Pilot*, which he found in the ship's library, and illustrated them with sketches. His use of these notes for the *Wild Cat*'s

voyage down the English Channel make it such an accurate account that a sailor could use those chapters of *Peter Duck* as a guide to navigation.

An earlier experience inspired *Wild Cat*'s hazardous duel in the fog with the *Viper*. On his way home from the Baltic just after war broke out in 1914, his ship made a long evasive detour up the coast of Norway, to dodge a pack of German destroyers known to be coming south from the North Cape. The passengers were told to make sure that no light whatever showed from portholes or windows. Ransome described how 'there came a moment when, ourselves hardly moving, we became aware of a group of four or five vessels moving southwards very fast, showing no masthead or navigation lights but not so well blacked-out as our own vessel had been by combined amateur and professional efforts'.

The *Wild Cat* made hardly any noise at all, hardly as much noise as the wind blowing over soft grass.

But suddenly John, in the bows, held up his hand. Susan signalled to Peggy. Peggy to Nancy. Everybody froze. There was no doubt about it. Somewhere in the fog, close to them, was the creak of steering-gear. Everybody knew that it was not the steering-gear of the *Wild Cat*. Then, away to leeward, came the noise of a wooden block on a slack rope, tapping a mast. Then the noise of men's voices, angry, muffled.

Titty looked at Peter Duck. He was not so much steering as holding the steering-wheel so that it should not move the millionth of an inch. He was not going to trust to oil alone to keep it quiet. The *Wild Cat* moved on, slowly, slowly. The muttering that, when they had first heard it, had sounded near the bows, sounded now astern.

'Them,' Titty whispered to herself. 'It must be them.'

The Channel, the tunnyfishers off Finisterre, and the distant coast of Spain described in *Peter Duck* were all part of Ransome's experience. But he never went to the Caribbean. That part of the story owes something to R.L. Stevenson's *Treasure Island*, but much more to a book by one of Ransome's great heroes, E.F. Knight, *The Cruise of the Alerte, the Narrative of a Search for Treasure on the Desert Island of Trinidad*. A true story, first published in 1905, it was reprinted in 1952 with an introduction by Arthur Ransome himself.

E.F. Knight had the health, energy and money to grab the chances of adventures which Ransome could only write about longingly. Knight heard a story of plunder from Peruvian churches which was buried by pirates on a volcanic island long ago in the 1820s, and vouched for by a Russian Finn with a deep scar on his cheek who (like Peter Duck in more ways than one) had seen the stuff buried and had a map

'OUR CAMP ON TRINIDAD' FROM E.F. KNIGHT,
THE CRUISE OF THE ALERTE

to prove it. He became as fidgety as Captain Flint, and
organized an expedition to search for it. His preparations
were rather more complete than the two toy spades which
Captain Flint picks up in an ice-cream shop in Cowes:

'What do you want those spades for?' asked Roger, when
the ices had been paid for, and they were all hurrying out
into the street.

'There isn't a spade in the ship,' said Captain Flint. 'And
I've only just noticed it. Ridiculous. And I thought I'd
fitted her out with everything.' And he strode down the
middle of the street carrying his paper parcel.

E.F. Knight, on the other hand, took a crew of fourteen in
his sixty-four-foot yawl *Alerte*, a stout lifeboat, with extra
water tanks, and everything a treasure-hunter could possibly
want: 'a complete set of boring apparatus, a Tangey hydraul-
ic jack capable of lifting twelve tons, a portable forge and
anvil, two of Messrs Piggot's large emigrant tents, wire-

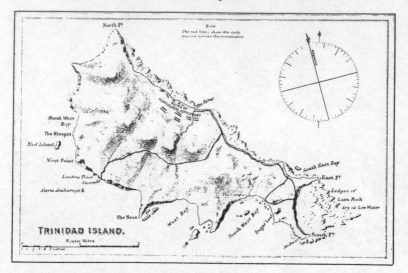

TRINIDAD ISLAND.

E.F. KNIGHT'S TRINIDAD COMPARED WITH ARTHUR
RANSOME'S CRAB ISLAND

fencing to keep off the landcrabs, a few gardeners' tools and seeds of quick-growing vegetables, taxidermic gear with a view to the rare seabirds that breed on the island, medical stores, surgical equipment, fishing tackle'.

On a grimmer note, for there was talk of rival expeditions fitting out, each member of the crew was provided with a Colt's repeating rifle, and 'the Duke of Sutherland kindly lent us one of Bland's double-barrelled whaling guns . . . a quick-firing and formidable weapon, discharging steel shot, grape, shell, and harpoons, and capable of sending to the bottom any wooden vessel'. Knight was not going to need a waterspout to erase competitors. 'I think the sight of the gun inspired some of my crew with ideas almost piratical. I have heard them express the opinion that it was a shame to have such a gun lying idle on board, and that an opportunity ought to be found of testing its powers.'

How similar were the two islands? Ransome's Crab Island is sited much farther north than E.F. Knight's Trinidad, which is off the coast of Brazil. But it cannot be coincidence that he makes Crab Island extremely close to the fertile Caribbean island of Trinidad. Surely this must be a private joke, a play on the fact that there are two Trinidads. E.F. Knight's real *desert* island of Trinidad, in case anyone is in a mood for treasure-hunting, lies at Lat. 18° South, Long. 30° West. Both it and Crab Island were volcanic, prone to landslips, and infested by landcrabs. 'The loathsome land-crabs might well be the restless spirits of the pirates them-

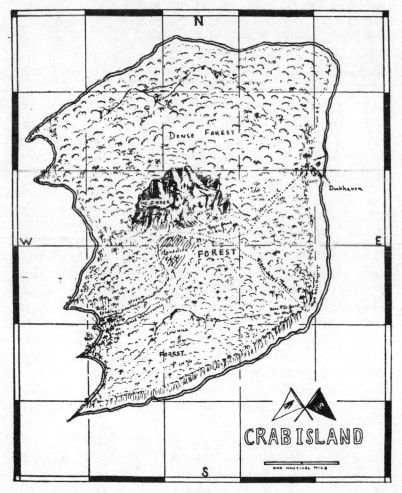

selves, for they are indeed more ugly and evil and generally more diabolical-looking than the bloodiest pirate who ever lived,' wrote Knight. The young Peter Duck agreed heartily: 'I hadn't the tonnage of Roger there, and I didn't like the look of those crabs . . . running sideways and lifting themselves and clapping their clippers, and goggling at me with those eyes of theirs.'

Peter Duck himself, of course, was Captain Sehmel, the Ancient Mariner who helped Ransome to sail around the Baltic in *Racundra*, although 'Their Own Story' suggests that he also owed something to the wherryman who shared Ransome's winter pike-fishing holidays. One of the best things about Ransome's story is the way Captain Flint, his sensible Uncle-self quite lost in the excitement of the treasure-hunt, and the rock-steady Peter Duck interact. 'Not so fast, Cap'n, not so fast,' Peter Duck cautions him as he hurries on regardless of danger, only to find himself during the last dreadful days wishing a thousand times that he had never come to look for the treasure. Still, his crew proves a comfort:

> 'Bringing the lot of you right over here. You just don't know what might have happened.'
>
> 'But we'd have wanted to come anyway,' said Titty.
>
> 'You ought to be jolly pleased now,' said Nancy. 'Think of the chapter you can put into the next edition of *Mixed Moss*.'
>
> 'It's much more of a treasure than just an old book,' said Roger, 'and you were very pleased about that.'
>
> 'It's what you always wanted to do,' said Peggy, 'and now you've done it.'
>
> 'And we've had a grand voyage,' said John. 'We'll remember it all our lives.'
>
> 'And it isn't over yet,' said Nancy.
>
> 'And nothing's really wrong that can't be mended,' said Susan.

Nancy, as usual, gets two remarks in to every one of the others.

Most of *Peter Duck* was written high in a tower room in the Altounyans' Aleppo home, and read out as it was written to the eager children, a situation startlingly like that of 'Their Own Story', and one which Ransome sometimes found distinctly odd. 'Ernest and Dora are on good form,' he wrote to his mother, 'and the children are good as usual, but I must say it seems a little queer now, after two years of living with them all in *Swallows and Amazons* and *Swallowdale*, to meet them once more as actual human beings running about. My lot seem the solider, but Ernest's are very nice, and eager to know "what is going to happen to us next?" '

In another letter, he mentions that 'Titty A.B. is working hard helping to produce pictures for the new book. She is most comically like her imaginary self. Ditto Roger. The others have all rather shot up in years.' The idea of doing the pictures for *Peter Duck* himself was part of its special character as a story which the children had made up themselves. This is why there is a note on its title page: 'Based on Information Supplied by the Swallows and Amazons and Illustrated Mainly by Themselves.' Most of the information had come in those letters answering this request for ideas, and here was the able-seaman busily working away at the pictures. Taqui remembers Ransome's own drawing technique: 'He usually shirked drawing faces and got over that difficulty with back views of shaggy heads of hair or hats – but he was meticulous in drawing endless graded lines in Indian ink for fog scenes.'

The Ransomes returned to England and Low Ludderburn in the spring of 1932. He made a trip to Lowestoft to check that his description of the harbour would be correct. Back in the Lake District, he went to Barkbooth and took photographs, 'hollywoods', of the Kelsall boys and the Hudson girls. 'Colonel Kelsall devised a lovely capstan for them,' he wrote in his diary. They also built rickety bunk-beds out of old doors, on which Peggy and Joan acted Susan and Peggy. Although originally meant as a joke, the *Peter Duck* drawings were such a success that Ransome's publishers suggested he should illustrate all his future books. He did so, and

169

eventually replaced the Clifford Webb drawings in *Swallows and Amazons* and *Swallowdale* with his own.

Now the books are inseparable from the drawings, although some foreign editions have found their own illustrators. Looking through a few of them, I liked their different interpretations of the maps and the boats. The attempts at faces for the characters made me realize how wise Ransome was to specialize in back views. Most bizarre of all was to see the original illustrations appear backwards through the Japanese editions, and to see Ransome's careful maps festooned with columns of oriental characters. At the same time, it struck me that there was something almost oriental about Ransome's drawings. They look very like the pictures in the children's story books which he had bought in China, presumably to help him learn a little Chinese, and which are still in the collection of his books at Abbot Hall, Kendal.

Motto for the whole book:- Let it Rip!

'Don't hold it in,' said Roger. 'Just let it rip' (advising Nancy on seasickness).

Begin after a shipwreck . . . as they drift about on rafts, barrels, etc . . . Gibber . . . with oil can . . . Parrot let out of cage to give it a chance flies off into the night . . . Woe . . . but Roger sings out that it must mean that they are near land.

Evgenia suggests Chinese background . . . Roger getting into trouble for lubricating prayer wheel to get rid of its squeak.

Chinese she-pirate . . . good English . . . missionary-educated and graduating from an American university . . .

It was thanks to Evgenia, it seems from reading these early notes for *Missee Lee*, that I got my favourite Ransome book. Like *Peter Duck*, it is pure romance, not pinned in time and reality at all. But Ransome *had* been to China, in 1926, and the book he wrote about the political situation there, *The Chinese Puzzle* (1927), describes warlords as ruthless as Wu and Chang – or Missee Lee and her father. 'They all say they are good, but who can tell the sex of a crow? All bad flesh smells alike.' His private journal was more frank: 'Wellington Koo – the most detestable little worm I have ever seen. Oily with a weak, cruel, uncertain scratch of a mouth, swollen heels to his jaws, wide eyes well practised in lack of expression, a poisonous little maggot of a man.' General Yang had 'the face of a clever ogre who has forgotten to shave'. Did Wu Pei-fu, an 'ancient-minded man', a poet and a Confucian scholar, as well as the leading bandit of the Northern Front, add colour to Missee Lee's background? And W.W. Yen, who had, in the middle of his traditional Chinese house, 'a perfectly English study'?

The model for Missee Lee was the wife of the politician Sun Yat-sen and a political figure in her own right after his death. She was educated by missionaries and then in America, just as the provisional outline for Missee Lee suggested. Ransome tells us that he talked to her 'in a flat full of cherry blossoms and baskets of flowers, no doubt greetings at the Chinese New Year. She is the most charming little woman, quite young, I suppose well under 30, with an eager expression, eyes that light up easily, not a great but a straight brain, happier in devotion than in for example unravelling any complicated political situation.' Mrs Sun Yat-sen told him that she hoped to visit England, and talked of Western culture. Only a year later her political fortunes had changed, and she was an exile. He met her again when he went to Russia in 1928.

Because it was New Year, Ransome saw the Dragon processions in the streets of Hankow, and made good use of them as the captives' way of escape in *Missee Lee*. He also noted the cage-birds everywhere, and told a story about a bird-loving Yangtse River skipper who could easily have been Chang. There were apparently two or three miles of the river where rival bandits shot at passing boats. When they reached them,

The old skipper remarked, 'Now gentlemen, we join the

canaries.' You see, he had armour-plated the bit of deck where he kept his bird cage . . . and there we sat, admiring his birds, while he rang for full speed ahead, and the engines did their damnedest, and the whole boat quivered with their efforts, and ping, ping, ping from the banks until the danger point was passed, when the old bird went along, peeking over the side to see the damage done, accompanied by the Chinese bosun, who had already stirred up a pot of paint, and mixed some putty, and was presently covering the holes and dints, so that the marksmen on shore would lose face when the condition of the steamship was reported down river.

Ransome had a missionary aunt, Edith Ransome, whom he visited while he was in China. He mentions to his mother that they were 'waited on by an ecstatically grinning old Chinese woman who evidently adores Aunt Edie'. She sounds very like Miss Lee's faithful amah.

Despite all this material, he very nearly gave up the book after six weeks' work on it. 'She has good points, but she is not yet ripe. She is too fantastic to be done before she has rooted herself in reality.' But slowly and surely Missee Lee came to life. Her background became Newnham College, Cambridge. Ransome wanted her to cox the college boat, and have a rudder on the wall of the room which was like 'walking out of Asia into Europe'. Although the ex-Newnhamites he asked told him that the college eight would have existed, they felt that it was not usual for Newnham's coxes to collar the rudder at the end of the season. So Missee Lee played hockey instead. 'My father could never understand hockey,' she tells Roger, and points to the Chinese characters added to her team photograph. 'That means "Breakers of hearts and shins".' No, that was not in the book. I found it in Ransome's notes, one of the many extra, unknown details which helped him feel so assured about his characters. It meant that he knew more about them than his readers did.

In some cases, however, he knew less. Like John, he

remembered the old-fashioned Latin gender rhymes which he wanted to use in Missee Lee's classroom 'as in a dream'. They were no longer included in Latin grammars. At last he discovered that his fishing friend Francis Hirst still knew the whole of 'Common are to either sex/Artifex and opifex' by heart (which shows what a useful rhyme it is). Hirst also produced an ancient family copy of Kennedy's *Latin Primer* which had written on its flyleaf both the Latin and the English curses on borrowers. Ransome decided to make Roger's initial crime not lubricating a prayer wheel but writing in Missee Lee's book.

Hic liber est meus
Testis est deus
Si quis furetur
Per collum pendetur
Like this poor cretur

'Who wrote in this book?' asked Miss Lee, sitting down at the table and opening the dictionary on her slanting desk.

'I did,' said Roger, very red indeed. 'I'm very sorry. I did it without thinking.'

'Not Latin,' she said, 'that last line, but velly good.'

'Our chaps always put it in,' said Roger, whose face was like sunshine breaking through clouds. 'I thought you'd just forgotten to finish it.'

The book was growing, he wrote to Margaret Renold in February 1941:

like a snowball . . . the stuff is piling up, but I am still much bothered over the intricate girder business of the skeleton which at present it lacks, except for a head and a tail. Lovely head . . . Elegant tail . . . but suet pudding in the middle. But that will soon come right . . . The scene of the pirate chief airing his singing lark while the pirates are set to catch grasshoppers for it (true to life) . . . the scene of the Dragon processions (which I watched at Hankow) . . . the dreadful burning of the *Wild Cat* . . . Miss Lee's back-sliding from her duty to her father's spirit, starting back for Cambridge and an academic career, but recalled to the path of virtue and piracy by the sound of the twenty-two gongs that show her position and dignity have been usurped.

The Latin material was vital. It gave Miss Lee a motive for keeping her prisoners alive: to make her own Camblidge on Dragon Island. This gave the book a sound central portion, much embellished by Roger's academic leadership. After all, it was originally designed as Roger's book, and for once Nancy is put down, in spite of a brave try on their first introduction to Missee Lee: ' "In for it now," said Nancy, confident once more now that the moment had come. "Look here, John. She's a she-pirate. Let me do the talking." '
After the first Latin lesson her humiliation is complete:

Miss Lee made up her mind to do the best she could with her uneven class.
'I think Loger will go to top,' she said. 'He will sit here. Then John. John had better lead Latin Grammar till he lemembers it. Then Tittee. She was all long about the second declension but she knows the first. Then . . .' She looked despairingly at the three others . . . 'Su-San, Nansee and Peggee . . . Never mind. They will lead glammar hard and we will do tlanslation all together. They will soon pick up.'
'Just try Roger in French,' said Nancy, one-time leader, but now at the bottom of the class . . .
'Flench,' said Miss Lee, 'is not a classical language.'

When Captain Flint joins the class he makes 'howler after howler'. One of them was a private joke. He declines big,

174

THE LITTLE DRAGON LEAVES THE YAMEN

bigger, biggest as magnus, magnior, magnissimus. Arthur
Ransome made the same mistake when he took the Rugby
scholarship exam as a boy – and failed it.

Although Captain Flint's Latin improved when he set his
mind to it, he remained a careless man. An observant Brownie
patrol noticed eight mistakes in his famous S.O.S. Ransome
sent a despairing letter to his publisher.

Curse and confound Captain Flint. It isn't the first time that
fellow's carelessness has got me into trouble. What's to be
done? I have corrected the original, and should like a new
block made at Captain Flint's expense, damn him. Or, if
there is no time for that, remove the title from under the
illustrations and print in very small type the following note:
This is not the original S.O.S which is somewhere in China.
Captain Flint had to make a copy of it for his book. While he
was doing so Roger was playing the penny whistle and
somebody else was not doing any harm just fingering
Captain Flint's accordion. He says that is why there are at
least eight mistakes in the signals. Really of course his

beastly carelessness. N.B. I do hope you'll manage the block in time for the reprint. Fry, frizzle and broil that fellow Flint. What's the use of my taking trouble when he goes and lets me down like this?

CAPTAIN FLINT'S S.O.S. — THE FIRST EDITION

I found a first edition of *Missee Lee* and compared the original version with the corrected one. Here they both are, so that readers can see if they are as hawk-eyed as those Brownies were.

CAPTAIN FLINT'S S.O.S. – THE CORRECTED VERSION

XII

The Mastodon's Lair

'I have a really gorgeous idea for a book,' wrote Ransome to his publisher in January 1936. 'Swallows only. No Nancy or Peggy or Captain Flint. But a GORGEOUS idea with a first-class climax . . . Lovely new angle of technical approach and everything else I could wish for. So I breathe again. I was really afraid I'd done for myself or rather for these stories by uprooting but I haven't.' The uprooting from the Lake District to East Anglia, far from doing for the stories, produced two excellent and completely individual books: *We Didn't Mean to Go to Sea* and *Secret Water*.

The Ransomes rented Broke Farm, Levington, on the northern bank of the River Orwell. 'From the upper room in which I worked,' Ransome wrote in a later (still unpublished) part of his autobiography,

I could see the river and the mouth of Levington Creek, with Harwich Harbour and in the distance Landguard Point and the open sea. There was thus a time in the day when the sun was over a sea horizon and I was able to take observations with my sextant, plot position lines and place us more or less correctly on the map. We could see steamers on their way to and from Ipswich, and the Danish butter boat coming in from Esbjiorg, and the mail steamers between Harwich and the Hook, and always a smack or two dredging for oysters or trawling.

As he sat looking over to the tiny port of Pin Mill where his new boat, the *Nancy Blackett*, had her mooring, it was hardly surprising that the idea for *We Didn't Mean to Go to Sea* came to him. Roger Altounyan told me that when his father Ernest Altounyan and Arthur Ransome were sailing together as young men their anchor had dragged one night, and they had found themselves drifting out to sea. Ransome did much more than recall that alarming early experience. He let himself and a crew, a man called Herbert-Smith, drift out to the Beach End Buoy in the *Nancy Blackett*, just as the Swallows did in Jim Brading's *Goblin*, and make for Holland. The voyage turned out to be even more like that of the Swallows than Ransome had bargained for. Herbert-Smith became extremely seasick and stayed below on his bunk throughout the voyage. After spending all night, like John, at the tiller, Ransome was relieved to 'sight the glimmer of the West Kapelle Light after leaving North Hinder', and to find 'that, steering as the children in my story steered, we should indeed reach the Deurloo Channel, and so come to the mouth of Flushing harbour'.

I am sure Ransome enjoyed that single-handed voyage. Nowhere is John more exactly like his creator than at the helm of the *Goblin* at night.

If anybody could have seen his face in the faint glimmer from the compass window, he would have seen that there was a grin on it. John was alone in the dark with his ship, and everybody else was asleep. He, for that night, was the Master of the *Goblin*, and even the lurches of the cockpit beneath him as the *Goblin* rushed through the dark filled him with a serious kind of joy. He and the *Goblin* together. On and on. On and on. Years and years hence, when he was grown up, he would have a ship of his own and sail her out into wider seas than this. But he would always and always remember this night when for the first time ship and crew were in his charge, his alone.

In Flushing, Ransome noticed jellyfish and crabs in the

179

lock, and had a good cup of coffee with 'Pilot Smit and his wife in their very clean and jolly little kitchen'. The pilot found him a young Dutch crew (Herbert-Smith had gone back on a steamer to Harwich, just as Commander Walker nearly did) and they explored the coast of Holland for a few days before sailing back home. 'I remember meeting a square-rigged vessel at dawn, a grain ship making north for her home in the Baltic,' Ransome wrote. She appeared, like Smit's Pilot Ship no. 7, in his story:

> 'In ballast,' said Daddy. 'See how high she is out of the water. She'll have left her grain at Ipswich. She'll have come round the Horn from Australia, and now she's going home.'
> 'So are we,' said Titty.

It is not just the accurate background which makes *We Didn't Mean to Go to Sea* such a good book; it also has that 'lovely new angle of technical approach' which Ransome tackled so enthusiastically. Its world is the closed-in shipboard of the *Goblin*. There is no counterplot, none of the usual diversions and distractions that normally flesh out Ransome's skeletons. It is all a matter of character, of John thinking harder than he has ever had to in his life, of Susan triumphing over her native panic and standing beside him to protect the younger two. If any single chapter had to be chosen to show Ransome's brilliance as a story-teller, it ought to be Chapter XII of *We Didn't Mean to Go to Sea* – 'A Cure for Sea-sickness'. Roger and Titty are in the cabin, draining Knight on *Sailing* in the sink and cheering up a little, unaware that overhead the intense drama of John's inch-by-inch struggle towards the mast to take in a reef is being played out, hearing only Susan's desperate shriek as she sees him apparently washed overboard. Phew, as Arthur Ransome used to say.

> 'Where's John?' said Roger, scrambling out on all fours, and tumbling head first into the cockpit.

By the time he had picked himself up, John had swung his legs over the coaming.

'Sorry, Susan,' he said. 'It's all right. You steered awfully well. Look here. It's all right now. Nothing's happened . . .'

'John! Oh, John!' said Susan.

'What happened?' said Roger.

'Nothing happened,' said John. 'I slipped. The life-line works beautifully. I'd have been all right even if I had gone overboard.' With hands that shook a little in spite of nothing having happened, he untied the rope he had knotted round his middle, coiled it carefully and put it away in the rope locker.

Titty, climbing out, looked from John to Susan and from Susan to John. She was just going to ask a question, but did not ask it. She felt that the ship was suddenly full of happiness. John was grinning to himself. Susan was smiling through tears that did not seem to matter.

Forget Ransome the sailor, the widely travelled journalist, the grown man nostalgic for his lost childhood. The real secret of his lasting importance is that he was a genuine craftsman at his chosen art of story-telling. The years which he spent in London before the First World War were a long apprenticeship in literature. He knew exactly what he was doing when he turned to writing his novels for children, for novels they really are.

To understand what was in Ransome's mind it is worth turning to his *A History of Story-Telling*, a book which he wrote when he was only twenty-five years old. It is a bad title. It sounds as if it is going to be a history of story-tellers, a collection of pen portraits of the great. In fact, as its sub-title says, it is a study of the development of narrative, and shows a very shrewd grasp of what great writers like Honoré de Balzac, Edgar Allan Poe and Guy de Maupassant were trying to achieve in the development of the story. Take an Edgar Allan Poe story to bits, he suggests. Work backwards from its solution and 'follow the mind of the architect . . . We can watch Poe refusing the slightest irrelevance, and at the same time artfully piling up detail on detail in exactly that order best calculated to keep the secret, to heighten the curiosity, to disturb the peace of the reader's mind, and to hold him in suspense until the end.'

Or consider Maupassant: 'He allows no abstract discourses on the psychology of his characters: he does not take advantage of their confessions. Their psychology is manifested in things said and in things done'; just as, time and again, we know what Ransome's own characters are feeling, not because he has told us, but because he has shown us.

The pilot and Daddy looked at each other, touched mugs and drank. Then the pilot turned to John.

'Your good health, Herr Capten. I am proud to have pilot your vessel into Flushing. I will remember it all my life. Your health, Herr Capten.'

John turned a very deep red under his sunburn, spluttered, caught his father's gravely smiling eyes and said, 'Thank you very much.'

The next minute Daddy was talking to the pilot about tides. Then he turned to John. 'What charts have you aboard?'

'Only English ones,' said John. 'Harwich to Southampton.'

Daddy's eyes flickered, but he only said, to the pilot, 'I suppose I can buy a North Sea chart in the harbour.' Then he turned to the others and asked, 'When did you last have something to eat?'

Ransome's books never pall because no two of them are the same. They are never churned out to a formula. Each one is a unique construction, with its own individual emphasis; sometimes on characters, sometimes on action, sometimes a traditional quest, sometimes a mystery to be solved. The twelve books are in themselves an education in the art of story-telling.

★

Our last journey in search of Ransome country was to Suffolk, late in April. We went through Colchester, then turned
off the B1456 south of Ipswich at Chelmondiston and drove
down a narrow winding lane to Pin Mill. A few dozen houses, a
couple of yacht chandlers, Harry King's boatyard and the Butt
and Oyster Inn are really all there is to Pin Mill, yet it gave
Ransome some of the happiest years of his life. He and Evgenia
had a much more sociable time there than they had had in the
Lake District. They watched their friends' boats sail in and out,
and went off for weekends with some of the local 'web-footed
youngsters' to crew for them.

I walked into the boatyard, past an avenue of high-and-dry
keels being freshened up for the coming season, to see if
anybody there remembered Arthur Ransome. Harry King had
built *Selina King* and *Peter Duck*. His son Sam, now himself
retired, remembered Ransome with affection. 'Huge fellow,
he was. Seventeen stone. He'd come over if we were lifting
something and say, "Here, let me put my weight on".' *Selina
King* was the second biggest boat their yard had ever built, and
Ransome spent a lot of time watching every stage of the
process.

I asked Sam to show me the famous Alma cottage, where the
Walkers stayed at Pin Mill, and where Jim Brading's head fell
forward on the table before he had a chance to eat the pea
soup and mushroom omelette he liked best of all Miss
Powell's dishes. Sam told me that there had been a real
Mrs Powell, the sailmaker's wife, and, with her permission,
Ransome had put her and her cottage into the book just as
they were. The only trouble was that she had had to learn
how to make omelettes fast because fans were soon turning
up to sample them. Alma Cottage is not quite its old self. Now
traditional Suffolk pink instead of white, it has been converted
into three small cottages, one bow-windowed, and omelettes
are no longer for sale. Otherwise, little has changed. Yachts
are still at anchor, there is a Thames barge beside the hard, and
sailing dinghies and rowing boats pick their way through the
mooring buoys in search of adventure.

When I was in London, I had met Josephine Russell, sister of

George who had kept such a good log of the cruises of the Northern River Pirates. Their family lived at Broke Hall, next door to the Ransomes, at the time when *We Didn't Mean to Go to Sea* and *Secret Water* were being written. She and George met him, rather as the Swallows met Jim Brading, by helping him moor *Coch-y-bonddhu*, in which he had just rowed over from *Nancy Blackett* after a fine cruise from Brightlingsea.

'He treated us as equals right from the start, when he first asked us if we could catch a rope for him. He always assumed that we would know things, and be able to do things. It was a great compliment. And he was so polite to us – most unusual for a grown-up then. He talked very quietly, and rather precisely – but he was full of fun. He had such a humorous, ironic way of putting things.'

Ransome took them sailing in *Nancy Blackett*, and patiently taught them how to handle her. He was an excellent teacher, explaining things simply and straightforwardly, and treating his pupils with a respect they soon earned. 'They became valued allies,' he wrote later. 'Both had a natural genius for small boats, and whenever Evgenia was too busy with her garden to come to sea with me, George and Josephine, if not at school, could be counted on.' All his boats were designed to be sailed by a single-handed skipper, so he could afford to carry young and inexperienced crews. Once the cruising season was over, the children helped Ransome with winter work on *Nancy*, sanding blocks, repairing rigging and so on, while he read them stories or played the penny whistle.

'Do you remember the tunes of the sea shanties he liked best?' I asked Josephine, showing her a copy of the article on sea shanties he had commissioned such a long time ago from John Masefield.

'Show me to a piano,' she said, and we were swinging into 'Spanish Ladies' in no time. 'Oh yes,' she said, skilfully sight-reading 'Hanging Johnny' and 'Away to Rio', 'that's right. He liked "D'ye Ken John Peel" and "Cock o' the North" too.'

'Did he ever talk about the actual writing of the books?' I asked.

SUSAN REVEALED — AN UNUSED DRAWING FOR
SECRET WATER

Josephine had thought it would be rude to ask him too
much about his work, but she did remember his answer to
the 'Are they real children?' question.

'Composites', Ransome had said. 'They're a mixture. There were real children, but now they've become something quite different; they're from my head.' She had been struck by how real his characters were to him. 'He used to refer quite casually to what Dick or Dorothea would have thought about something that was happening to us. We liked the Ds. I know they were invented before we met him, but we felt quite like them.'

The most popular destination on their weekend cruises was Hamford Water, nine square miles of islands, creeks, marshes and lagoons just south of Harwich. George and Josephine often went with him in *Nancy Blackett*, towing *Coch-y-bonddhu* (which Ransome let them use as their own until they found another dinghy, the *Royal George*) and carrying the tiny tender to *Nancy*, the *Queen Mary*, on the foredeck. Another family, Colonel Busk and his wife, and their three children, Jill, Michael and John, often sailed there with them in their yacht *Lapwing*, towing their dinghy *Wizard*. *Lapwing* was the name of the missionary ship in *Secret Water*, and *Wizard* was that of the Swallows' borrowed dinghy. *Firefly*, the Amazons' dinghy, was in real life a seven-ton sloop, belonging to other Pin Mill friends, the Clay family.

Henry Clay, an economist, wrote for the *Manchester Guardian*, like Ransome. He had four children, Gabriel, Jim, Helen and John. Was Jim Clay Jim Brading? His son Jamie suspects that he was. *Firefly*, still owned by the Clay family, was very like *Nancy Blackett*, and Jim Clay was just going up to Oxford at the time he met Ransome in 1935. Jim himself believes that the character was more of a mixture, owing something to another keen sailor and friend of Ransome's, Dick Tizard. But he does remember how impressed Ransome was to discover that on the family's voyage to Holland and back it had been the four children who had taken charge of the sailing. Perhaps hearing about that adventure, and his own memories of drifting out to sea, gave Ransome the idea for *We Didn't Mean to Go to Sea*, first mentioned in a letter in January 1936, and dedicated to Mrs Henry Clay.

Secret Water was dedicated to the Busks. Undoubtedly, Daisy, Dum and Dee were modelled on the Busk children.

If anybody had looked from an aeroplane they would have seen something like a floating island moving slowly with the tide in the middle of Secret Water. It was a smooth, oily calm, without a breath of wind. *Wizard* had tied up alongside *Firefly*. Nancy and Daisy, John and Dee, Titty and Dum, each couple in one of the tiny dinghies of the Eels, had thrown painters aboard one of the larger boats. The Mastodon with Roger had rowed round them all, and ended up by coming close under *Wizard's* stern. All six boats were close together. Food was being passed from boat to boat, and everybody was busy eating.

In real life, according to Josephine, such feasts might well end in a 'capsizing party', a popular occupation when the wind made sailing impossible. 'Our favourite anchorage', wrote Ransome, 'was in Kirby [Goblin] Creek, where we elders had our ships to ourselves, and the crews would be off in their little boats to set up a camp on Horsey Island. Tents sprang up. There were fires at night, and during the day, great exploration of all those intricate waters that lie hidden from the sea, behind the Naze.' In August 1937, jottings for a story appeared in his diary.

Muddy creeks . . . tidal . . . an island . . . like Walton Backwaters . . . a hut . . . a house . . .

Town children come to stay ? Callums
Local children . . . watch

The visitors know they are being watched but cannot see anybody. The locals show themselves when visitors have got into the dickens of a mess and are doing their best, but failing to get out of it . . . In the end, of course, it is the locals who are in a mess and the visitors somehow help them through.

The next stage the book reached was a brief synopsis for 'Marooned' or 'The Mastodon Boy'. There were to be only three local children, and no Amazons.

Story begins with the landing of the Swallows on one of the islands in Hamford Water. Commander Walker and Mrs Walker busy settling in at Shotley, and Commander Walker, to get rid of them for a week while the settling in is going on, borrows the *Goblin* and dumps them on the island [where he himself once spent a weekend as a boy] to do the best they can for themselves when really marooned and on a desert island. They have masses of tinned food, milk, etc., a rope, an axe, a saw, and that's that.

They settle in and making their camp, and making the circuit of their island, they come upon the tracks of a mastodon, huge round prints in the mud.

As the mist rises after dawn, they see something moving on one of the other islands. They stick up a flagstaff. Can't find the mastodon prints, but while looking for them, they see the mastodon, a small boy, crossing the mud left at low tide between the other island and the mainland, walking funnily because he is wearing duckboards to prevent him sinking in the mud. They see him leave the duckboards and go off inland.

The next thing is a bit later in the day, when Roger as lookout sees the boy running like blazes across the low ground of the mainland, and then they see him no more. But, presently they see his pursuers, a boy and a girl, with an eager spaniel, 'a blood-hound' says Titty. The chase comes to the ditch, and presently reappears in a duckpunt, lands and comes up to the Swallows' camp, looking about them, taking opportunities of looking into tents, but while very polite and apparently friendly, saying nothing about the boy. The Swallows also say nothing. The others go, and are hardly out of sight when the Mastodon boy turns up from nowhere.

The boy explains (which is more than I can do) what is the meaning of the hunt. He stays to supper with them, and next day at high water they swim across to his island, and he shows them his lair, in the stern part of a derelict barge, most of which is already rotted away.

He accepts the idea of their marooning, and they accept his idea (whatever it is) and each work in with the other. He suggests a raft, and they set about building one. Also turns them on to fishing and laying eel lines. There is shooting, and he brings in a dead wild duck, which has fallen on his island and not been retrieved. Susan cooks it.

Another chase, in which Roger, as the boy doubles back along the ditch, becomes a red herring, and is pursued by the hunters, eventually dodging them by rolling in the mud till he is mud all over, and wallowing in the mud so that they pass close by without seeing him.

CLIMAX? The raft not quite complete when the weather comes hard from the north, and an exceptionally high tide swamps the island. They get up on the sea wall and work to finish the raft, and as the tide comes to the top of the wall, take to it, and with the ebb might have drifted out to sea if the boy had not managed to get a boat to them . . . The *Goblin*, with Commander Walker, comes to fetch them off, and finds swamped island and eventually rescues the lot. All hopelessly vague, but the business of the islands and the mastodon boy in his lair in the old barge does somehow seem promising.

Indeed it was, although the raft drifting out to sea was too like the last book. A few weeks later, the locals had become the Mastodon boy and the three Lapwings (not yet Eels) a heathen tribe, with totems and human sacrifices. The Swallows, given a boat at last, were no longer primarily marooned but surveying. This made a nice conflict between the two rival groups, and brought in the haunting psychological factor of loyalty to one's own gang. One of the reasons why *Secret Water* is the most elusive of all the books is that it seems to be working on several different levels. The many early drafts left their traces on the finished story, and there is yeast in the air. Perhaps the children are growing up. Nancy's secret conclave with Daisy puts a barrier between her and her old ally, John.

'Hullo! What happened?'

'Stuck really hard,' said Daisy. 'We just had to wait for the tide. It didn't matter. There was a lot to talk about.'

Both of them were smiling. It seemed to John almost as if they had been glad of the delay.

The necessary link between the upright map-making Swallows and the savage Eels were the Amazons. Almost regretfully, as if bullied a little, Ransome added a hand-written note to his typed synopsis: 'Nancy and Peggy (mainly N) hankering after excitement become more and more savage, and at the very end take charge *as* savages, and bring realism with the corroboree.'

As comic relief – very necessary in the highly charged atmosphere – Ransome brought on Bridget, highly conscious of her own dignity, and no longer the youngest in the family because Sinbad the ship's kitten comes too. She has missed most of the adventures but at last, to her delight, she comes face to face with savages.

'Who are you?' said Bridget, whispering, though there was no one else to hear, and then suddenly she guessed.

'Kara . . . kara . . . karabadangbaraka,' she stuttered.

'Akarabgandabarak,' said the girl instantly.

'Gnad,' said Bridget. 'Gnad . . . You're Daisy. He said you always said Gand by mistake.'

'He's said lots too much,' said Daisy.

The first view of Secret Water which our own expedition had was from Witch's Quay, a left-hand turn off the B1034 in Kirby le Soken, a little village just before Walton on the Naze. It is a private road, but the owner of the two houses at the very end of the quay let us drive along it. One of his houses is let as a holiday cottage, and would make a good base for anyone with a boat to explore the Backwaters, as they are known locally. The Witch's Cottage is still there, as black and thatched as Ransome describes it, but no longer rundown, and lacking a witch. Smoke rose from its brick chimney and it looked inviting and warm, but we did not want a roof over our heads. Supported by a new bo'sun, Jo Birley, just as keen a camper and sailor as Jane, we were planning to put our tents as close to the water as possible. Quay Lane was much too civilized for savages. We drove back and found a farmer who, as a special concession, let us camp right down beside the sea wall, opposite Mastodon Island and in sight of Swallow Island (or, in native parlance, opposite Skipper Island and in sight of Horsey Island).

We pitched our three tents, unpacked sleeping bags and clothes from the car, and made a safe, if unconventional, fireplace out of a rusty wheelbarrow top. Daisy disappeared into her tent to read, Tilly and Ellen raced up the sea wall to see the lie of the land, and Susie practised getting into her pyjamas. Jo and I followed on up the sea wall, and found that we were looking at an ocean of mud. The tide was right out. Grubby tussocks of thin grass sprouted from the mud. Tiny streams meandered between them, promises of the flood to come. A man in a guernsey walked briskly past, wished us good evening, and crossed three rickety wooden bridges between the islands to a cockleshell dinghy, which he rowed rapidly over to Skipper Island. Two girls were toiling away in an even smaller dinghy, standing up with their oars for some reason, and making very little headway in the creek, as both wind and tide were against them. They finally tied up the dinghy where the man had embarked, and disappeared.

Tilly and Ellen ran on to try out the wooden bridges for themselves, and named them: Creaky Causeway, the Big Dipper (it was *very* rocky) and Elephant Bridge.

Next morning we decided to cross the Red Sea and explore Horsey Island. In Ransome's day the 'King of Horsey Island' was David Haig-Thomas, a Greenland explorer. His wife 'Queen Nancy' (another Nancy?) was the daughter of a man called Bury with whom Ransome shot duck on the Nile when he was in Egypt. Their daughter still farms the island today. We got permission from her to cross the Wade, as the causeway from the mainland to the island is officially known, one afternoon.

'Low tide is at 16.37 today,' she told us. 'So you have a good two hours each side of that when the road will be passable.'

We turned off the Walton road down a track marked 'New Brick Mill Farm only. Dead End' and parked the car beside a wartime pillbox. The Wade still has its line of withies to mark the road when it is covered with water, but the four posts at its highest point have gone. There would be nothing today for the ship's baby and the ship's boy to perch on and hope for rescue, while Titty rallied them bravely from below.

'Look here, Bridgie,' said Titty. 'You know how to float. Well, you're going to. You'll just have to lie on your back and keep still and I'm going to swim you ashore. It's going to be easy as easy.'

'But I can't,' said Bridget. 'Not for as long as all that. Isn't anybody coming? You said they were coming. And what about Sinbad?'

'Roger'll take Sinbad. It'll be all right. And then we'll run and get dry, and everybody'll be awfully proud of you.'

'Would Susan let me?' said Bridget.

'Of course she would. And so would John. It isn't as if you were too young.'

192

34-6 *Orestes*, a possible model for the schooner *Wild Cat*, and Captain Sehmel (*right*) alias Peter Duck. *Below:* Ransome's political mission to China in 1928 gave him the background for *Missee Lee*.

37-9 *Above:* Pin Mill today, little changed from Ransome's drawing in *We Didn't Mean to Go to Sea*. The drawing in that book of a Dutch dog-drawn milk cart was inspired by this photo (*below right*), taken by Ransome's sailing friend Herbert Hanson. Other Pin Mill friends were Colonel Busk and his family (*below left*).

40-2 The Busk children became the Eels in *Secret Water* and the Busk
yacht, *Lapwing*, here at Pin Mill, kept her own name as the
missionary ship moored off Flint Island (*inset*). *Below:* young
friends of the Ransomes camping on Horsey (Swallow) Island in
Hamford Water.

43-5 *Top:* the author windsurfing in Kirby (Goblin) Creek, with Skipper (Mastodon) Island in the background. The trees to the left are the heronry. *Centre:* the black-thatched cottage at Witch's Quay is now a holiday house. *Below:* Daisy, Ellen, Tilly, Susie and the author follow in the Israelites' footsteps across the Wade to Horsey Island.

It looked a longish walk, perhaps three-quarters of a mile, and with a hard wind in our faces it felt even longer. At first it was exciting, with our sorties into the surrounding morass of soupy chocolate-coloured mud growing more and more daring. Then Susie sat fatly down in it, and I had to carry her. Daisy's new rubber boots, bought in Walton specially for the expedition, began blistering her heel. Ellen, doubtful from the start about the wisdom of the expedition ('The ship's baby was beginning to lose faith in the able-seamen'), looked nervously at the creeks full of water at each side of us, and talked of Egyptians.

An approaching land-rover made a welcome distraction. It gave the road an ordinary air, a solid feel. It stopped beside us, and the island's owner leaned out. She had met Ransome when he moored first the *Nancy Blackett* and later the *Selina King* in Kirby Creek. After the war he sailed there in *Peter Duck*, but she said he no longer brought children with him. Many of the boys he had known had been killed in the war. He never regained those cheerful, sociable sailing years based at Pin Mill, and the loss of young companions meant that his desire to write children's books dried up.

The land-rover drove away in a fountain of mud. We were past the half-way mark, a footing of concrete rubble between the receding rivers of water, and life began to look up. Tilly had discovered how warm the mud was by dipping her arms into it and squeezing it through her fingers. Wading through the deepest bits, it was hard to resist an urge to roll in it and turn into Eels ourselves.

At last we reached the island itself, and took shelter from the wind by the sea wall. The children didn't want to walk any farther, so I left them splatching on the beach with Jo, and headed along the sea wall to the Swallows' camp on the western shore of the island.

Horsey was larger and more wooded than I had expected. There were acres of rich pasture on which sheep and horses were grazing. I didn't see any buffaloes, but Titty had marked them on the other side of the island. It struck me as I walked along, watching the white sails of yachts beyond the meadows,

what a watery book *Secret Water* is. There is very little about the
places that the Secret Archipelago Expedition discover, it is
almost all about the ways they get to them – rowing, sailing,
splatching or merely wading through the mud. The Swallows'
camp at the landing to the west of the island looked very like
Ransome's drawing of it, even to the clumps of hawthorn trees
to which they tied the older, rope-slung tent. There is a lake
there now, made by an enlargement to the stream which runs
inside the sea wall. Otherwise the muddy flats and the landing
hard are unchanged.

The journey back across the Wade (still safely uncovered)
was much more successful. Susie skipped ahead with Jo.
Tilly and Daisy raced past them to explore the pillbox, and
I walked in a more leisurely way with Ellen, who felt she
could afford to play with the mud and collect cockleshells
now that we were homeward bound. Before, like Titty I
think, she had been 'looking straight above her and seeing
not hawks or larks or infinite blue sky, but a few feet of
swirling water over her head, and the red painted bottom and
centreboard of a little boat'.

We could find no path to Sinbad Creek as we went back
to the main road. A look at the official map showed why.
Accurate as Ransome usually was, he had invented it.
Originally, Titty, Roger and Bridget spent their precious
time talking to a man at the little yacht club which *is* there.
Sinbad's Creek was author's licence, to improve the story.

So back to our camp by Skipper Island. We were not as
efficient at housekeeping as Susan, and had absolutely nothing on which to cook the sausages, until Jo had the happy
thought of pushing tent pegs through a few at a time and
hanging them over the side of the wheelbarrow top, which
then worked like the walls of an oven. While she was reading
the children the next chapter of *Secret Water*, I rigged up the
windsurfer and took it for a sail.

The tide had come in now, and I could get right round
Bridget Island (local name: the Honey-pot) and see the
Swallows' camp from the water. I could also see Mastodon
Island well, but as it was inhabited now, by the man who had

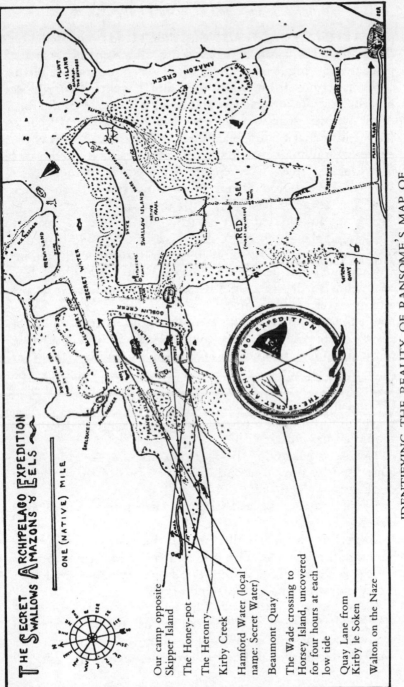

IDENTIFYING THE REALITY OF RANSOME'S MAP OF SECRET WATER

Our camp opposite Skipper Island

The Honey-pot

The Heronry

Kirby Creek

Hamford Water (local name: Secret Water)

Beaumont Quay

The Wade crossing to Horsey Island, uncovered for four hours at each low tide

Quay Lane from Kirby le Soken

Walton on the Naze

passed us on the day we arrived, I didn't land on it. Being on the water gave a much better sense of the mystery of the place than seeing it from the land. It was quite impossible to sort out islands from mainlands until I went in very close indeed. The Wade was now an ocean, without even the tops of the withies to show where we had been walking. I could see the little black cottage at Witch's Quay, and far away the clutter of buildings that marked Walton itself. A yacht came into Goblin Creek from Secret Water (local name: Secret Water!) and moored. Then an amazing raft on four huge pontoons zoomed past me, with the man from the island sitting in an old car-seat attached to its stern, casually foot-steering with an oar lashed on as a tiller. He waved. I waved, and, carried away by admiration for the craft, fell in. It was much warmer than Coniston Water, but after a few more runs to dry myself, I decided to go and see how the sausages were getting on.

On the way back to the camp, I found a large bunch of keys. Perhaps they belonged to the islander. I walked as close to his landing as I could, and signalled. He came to the door of his wooden hut and looked out. When he saw the keys, he nodded vigorously and shouted that he would come over in the morning.

Next morning he did come over, and suggested that we should all pay him a visit.

'Is he the Mastodon Boy grown up?' whispered Daisy, quite used by now to seeing older versions of the Ransome characters.

'I expect so,' I said, as I strapped Susie into my buoyancy jacket.

Masterfully he marshalled us into his own slightly leaky boat, and the even smaller one which the two girls had left there. I offered to row it, but found there were no rowlocks. No wonder they had been standing up.

'Never mind. I'll tow you,' he said cheerfully.

We set off, wind and tide against us, making one yard headway for every two rowed, but landing safely on the other side. There was the raft I had admired yesterday, alongside an old landing-craft, a motor boat and a wooden cruiser, the *Patricia Ann*. The island itself is now a nature reserve, run by the Essex Naturalists' Trust, and is not normally open to the public. The heronry which the Swallows mapped is still there, but since the sea wall was breached by the floods of 1953, and the central lake became salt-water, the herons have left. Skipper Island used to be three separate islands until John Skipper built a sea wall round it in the eighteenth century, and it still falls into three parts, the heronry, the main part where the house and the boats are, and the low-lying flats to the north.

We walked round the grassy tracks that crisscross the island's impenetrable thickets of hawthorn and brambles, and climbed up the sixty-foot-high observation tower for a view of the countryside which would have helped the Swallows' mapmaking considerably. I realized how enormous Hamford Water is. Skipper Island alone covers eighteen acres, and the creeks and islands around stretched as far as we could see. Harwich looked startlingly close, with two white steamers beached like stranded whales under its cranes and davits.

While the three older children clung on to the back of the Mastodon's ancient tractor and helped him clear the undergrowth, Susie, the ship's baby, and I went for a walk around the boats. Just beyond the *Patricia Ann* we came across a huge wooden skeleton lying in the mud. A barge's bones. The *Speedy*? 'No,' said the Mastodon, who knew all about *Secret Water*. 'Those are the ribs of the *Alpha*. There was a chap called Sampson who owned the island in the 1940s. He went out wildfowling one night and his house caught fire. So he bought the *Alpha* and used her as a houseboat while he built another house. He had a yacht called *Secret Waters*, by the way.'

(A few weeks later, however, when I was talking to Jim Clay about his sailing days with Ransome, he told me that when he had sailed to Hamford Water and Kirby Creek in 1937 he had seen the hull of a Thames barge on the mud beside Skipper Island, with bare ribs at her bows and a cabin in her stern just like the *Speedy*. So there must have been a barge there before the *Alpha*.)

197

SPEEDY

Hoots of laughter came from the children. They were piled into the back of an extraordinary eight-wheeled open jeep which was careering across the grass with the Mastodon at the joystick (it didn't have a wheel). He took us all round the island in it on one of his regular patrols of the nature reserve. The contraption shot through the brambles, mashed down the reeds, and then drove straight up the sea wall, teetered on top, and tilted down the other side. We drove along a bank close by the creek tilted at forty-five degrees. Trying to sort out the screams of pleasure from those of terror, the Mastodon looked over his shoulder at the children, who were straining to keep away from the water.

'Don't worry, she floats,' he shouted.

It worked.

'Really?' they asked, and calmed down.

'Yes. Amphibian. You just put an outboard motor on the back or row her. Canadian toy, but they make them in Kent.'

We looked more closely at the smooth, waterproof body of the jeep.

'Can we try her out?' asked Tilly.

'Too windy today,' the Mastodon said firmly.

After we had inspected the new repairs to the breached dyke, we were invited into the Mastodon's lair for coffee and grog. It was very civilized now, with comfortable sofas, a record player and a modern bathroom. But we could tell that it was in spirit the old hull of the *Speedy* by the slightly barrel-shaped roof, the charts everywhere, and the orderly galley.

Having downed a couple of strengthening glasses of lemonade, Daisy came straight to the point.

'Where are your splatchers?' she asked.

The Mastodon led us to a near-by shed, full of useful and potentially useful objects – a mudcomber's treasure trove. He disappeared inside, and unhooked two rusty dusty objects from the wall. Splatchers. Hinged splatchers at that. We looked at them with awe as he explained that he had thought putting hinges on might help to break the suction created by the mud underneath them. It was answer enough. This was not only the Mastodon, but an older and wiser Mastodon. It was the best possible end to our quest.

SPLATCHERS

XIII

A Benefactor to Humanity

Although our travels had ended in Essex, there was still the final Ransome story to investigate. In a way, it proved to have the most interesting origin of all. *Great Northern?* was dedicated 'To Myles North, who, knowing a great deal of what happened, asked me to write the whole story'. I discovered that this was literally true. Without Myles North, we would not have the neatly rounded Ransome dozen. The saga would have ended with *The Picts and the Martyrs*.

After he had finished *Picts*, Ransome lost direction. He was now living at The Heald, looking over a lake full of ghosts, and knowing no young children. Evgenia, whom he called his 'Critic on the Hearth', was always outspoken in her criticism, and when he was younger he had found that useful. But she had thoroughly disapproved of *The Picts and the Martyrs*, and was equally discouraging about 'The River Comes First', a period piece of a quite different type from his usual books. It is the story of a gamekeeper on the River Beela, as a boy on the river, and then as a young man, interesting for its sense of history and feeling for fishing, but not at all what readers had come to expect from Ransome. After six chapters, he gave it up. 'God knows I am going to need a bit of encouragement,' he wrote to his mother in August 1943, 'if, in spite of local veto, I am going to write any more.'

At last he got it, from Major Myles North, who worked in East Africa for the Colonial Office. The correspondence began over matters of birds and fish. Ransome wanted some of the neck-feathers of the vulturine guinea-fowl, an African bird, because they looked exactly like tiny eels, elver, when tied as a fishing fly, and he thought that nothing could be tastier for salmon on their way up river – picky creatures, not really hungry at all – to chew on. (The full, very funny story of how he decided that 'Salmon Chew Gum' is told in *Mainly about Fishing*.) North sent him the feathers, and much more besides. 'I like the people you write about, and their quite remarkable "aliveness" and characterization. Given any set of circumstances, the reader knows just how Nancy or Roger or Susan would feel; they are real people, and such lively and nice ones at that.' His next letter, talking about the origin of Peter Duck, showed how intimately North knew the children:

> No reason at all why you shouldn't have brought him to life if you wished. In fact, I suspect you had to! And that something on the following lines happened: *Scene: Your Study (Enter gang of nephews & nieces.)*
> NNs: Look here, Captain Flint, we want a book about Peter Duck.
> Yourself: There is no Peter Duck. He's an invention of Titty's.
> NNs (menacingly): Who invented Titty?
> Yourself (trapped): Well, I suppose I did.
> NNs (in triumph): Right. Now you can go on and invent Peter Duck.

Pretty good, for someone who had not read 'Their Own Story'. North went on, full of enthusiasm for Ransome's effortless style, which he compared to Arthur Conan Doyle and John Buchan, praising the 'practicability which runs through all your stories and is one of their great charms. Everything works.' North was 'no expert' on sailing, although he had done some on Lake Windermere, and had once been round the Outer Hebrides in a twenty-foot sloop with an expert friend from Cambridge. The last part of this letter held pure gold:

Birds are my main hobby. You are clearly a birdman too: your descriptions of them show that. But as far as I know, you have not yet written a story which centres round a *wild bird* (which excludes parrots and pigeons). The other day, I was jolting along in a truck over some rather unattractive country in the hinterland of Cape Gardafui, and fell to thinking what sort of bird might fit into one of your stories. The result is attached. If you took it and moulded it and breathed life into it, would it "go"? Ornithologically, at any rate, I don't think there is anything that could be disputed.

I read 'the result', in North's clear, sprawling handwriting, marked with Ransome's own ticks of enthusiasm and occasionally overhasty No!s, with disbelief. In all essentials it was the plot of *Great Northern?*, written by a man for whom the Swallows, Amazons and Ds were as real as they were to Ransome, although he had not then read *Coot Club*. His egg-collector was more of a caricature: 'Like a proper egg collector he must be wearing a cap and plus fours and have protruding teeth and an acquisitive nose.' His plan to have Peter Duck and Bill turn up as the crew of the *Pterodactyl* was a little incredible. There was no young Gael. Otherwise, he gave Ransome not only the bones of a story but a wealth of ornithological detail including the unforgettable bird-hunters' proverb: 'What's hit's history, what's missed's mystery.' That is, he went on to explain, 'if you want to prove your bird beyond all doubt, you must shoot it.'

Best of all, perhaps, North's enthusiasm and evident faith in the *Swallows and Amazons* characters gave Ransome the confidence to start again. He wrote back to North thanking him, and they exchanged letters discussing such technicalities as nesting times and egg-blowing. The breeding habits of the Great Northern Divers did not suit Ransome's school-holiday setting, so for once there is no mention of time of year in the book. This is why, apart from the fact that Dick very nearly gets shot by the egg-collector, I have placed *Great Northern?* in the fantasy class of *Peter Duck* and *Missee Lee*.

...eryone wonder what the g.A. will say
...en she hears about this?

All now rush quickly, but quietly, down
...the loch, ~~which~~ is shining in the
...moonlight. They ~~are~~ too late ~~as just as~~
...ney arrive, they see a portable dinghy
...land on the islet. They ~~have~~ no boat
...handy in which to ~~follow~~ so they have
to wait & waylay the egg collector on
his return.

The interval, for Dick especially, is an
...nscious one, ~~owing~~ to his knowing that —

(a) Egg collectors often ~~too do~~ blow, or
...artly blow, their eggs ~~to~~ immediately
...make them lighter, & thus stronger, to
travel;

(b) An ~~ornithological~~ saying runs
"What's hit's history; what's missed,
mystery." i.e. if you want to prove your
...rd beyond all doubt, you must __shoot__
__t__.

However, no __shot__ is heard, and the
dinghy returns to ~~land~~ where the egg-
collector is duly ~~challenged~~. Dick opens
the egg box with ~~trembling~~ hands, and
~~finds~~ the two eggs unblown, & still warm.
So they are rushed off to the nest
& replaced there, & a few moments

A PAGE FROM MYLES NORTH'S SYNOPSIS OF
GREAT NORTHERN?

There was no longer a *Wild Cat* to sail in, of course, so Ransome provided the *Sea Bear*. She was an old Norwegian pilot vessel, modelled on the *Teddy*, heroine of one of Ransome's favourite books of epic voyages, Erling Tambs's *The Cruise of the Teddy*.

The climax of that story is when the *Teddy* is wrecked, and Tambs has to trust his son, the three-year-old 'mate', to perch on the reef and cling on to his eighteen-month old baby sister while he himself dives into the crashing surf to save his wife. When Ransome wrote an introduction for the first English edition of the book, he told Tambs that readers would want an exact description of the *Teddy*, inside and out. He found it very useful himself when he brought her to life again as the *Sea Bear*.

The collaboration was exactly what Ransome needed to produce another book. North proved to be an enthusiastic, well-informed and very intelligent supporter with whom he could bounce ideas backwards and forwards. 'If the diver story gets you going,' wrote North at one point, 'I shall regard myself as a benefactor to humanity, or at least to that part of humanity that really matters.' And so he was. *Great Northern?* got under way almost immediately. By December 1944, Ransome wrote to the Renolds that it had reached page 280,

> but awfully dull stuff. You can feel the immobility of lead in every line of it. But perhaps that is just as well, because it will make it less heartrending to pull it to pieces and rewrite it after getting a squint at the Hebrides to check the details, which are probably all wrong.

It was inevitable that Ransome's passion for exactitude would send him to the Hebrides himself. He does not seem to have been there before. He wrote letters to the *Stornoway Gazette* inquiring about hotels, and then a fishing friend, A.R. Wallace, suggested he stay at Wallace's brother-in-law's fishing lodge near Uig, on the Isle of Lewis. His first visit to the Dobsons at Uig Lodge was in May 1945, and he went

A NEW VIEW OF THE GREAT NORTHERN DIVER

again in July 1946 to make more sketches – Lou Langabhat, the head of Uig Bay, the Gorge down to the bridge and Loch Crummock above it – which give some clue to what was fiercely held to be a secret landscape. Long after *Great Northern?* was finished, he used to return to Lewis to fish for salmon, so Myles North had given him not only a book but a new place in which to feel at home.

As usual, Ransome did some careful background reading. C.C. Lynane's *Log of the Blue Dragon* (1910) was the story of a family's cruise round the Hebrides, and Osgood Mackenzie's *Hundred Years of Life in the Highlands* (1921) produced a blind piper and an eccentric laird who took a long time to don Highland dress. Mackenzie's best use for a Great Northern Diver was in the pot; 'better than three fat hens,' he remarked of a seventeen-pounder that he shot. Ironically, considering the number of record bags he mentions shooting, his last chapter is a regretful one on 'Vanishing Birds'.

I was half afraid when I unearthed the true story of *Great Northern?* that it might in some way discredit Ransome, but I think that if one looks at North's synopsis, and then considers how Ransome did indeed 'mould it and breathe life into it', it does the opposite. It shows his genius for construction and characterization, and profound feeling for what worked

205

and what didn't in North's plot. 'Great Auks and Guillemots! I never thought birds could be half such fun,' says Nancy, rising with typical generosity to the occasion. The old hand had not lost its cunning, even though it wrote despairingly at one stage: 'Page 195 and stuck again. I am TOO OLD.'

It was his last Swallows and Amazons book, a fact neatly symbolized by the final picture in it, 'Farewell to the Sea Bear', so curiously placed looking away from the text. But the real end to the story was not quite so neat. Myles North was raring to go again, with a really wild yarn in which the Coot Club take on their old enemy George Owden again. This time they are in Kenya, where George Owden has been sent as a 'bad lot', and where the Coots, 'perhaps Tom and the Twins', come out with Mrs Barrable to visit some friends, who have two children. They are to hunt for the legendary Nandi Bear on safari near Lake Victoria, where Mrs Barrable's friend keeps a cruising yacht. Despite the six-page synopsis and invitation to visit Kenya which North sent him, Ransome did not rise. He was busy with the two boats which gave him some very happy sailing in his later years, *Peter Duck* and *Lottie Blossom*. He prepared another book on fishing, and revisited the Hebrides, of which he grew increasingly fond.

BOILING WITH GRAYLING

He was also very much involved in the affairs of the Mariners' Library, an excellent series of seafaring books published by Rupert Hart-Davis, to which he was 'godfather and nanny'. Nothing was published without Ransome's approval, and many of the titles were included at his suggestion. He wrote introductions to six of the volumes, and his own *Racundra's First Cruise* became the thirty-eighth. It is clear that he put an enormous amount of time and trouble into reading suitable books, arranging for copies to be made available, and thinking over the general direction of the whole scheme. He refused any payment, but Rupert Hart-Davis, knowing he had always longed for the Complete Oxford English Dictionary, gave him a set as a present: 'They were all much-belated pieties,' wrote Ransome, 'and the republishing of those books gave me a very great deal of pleasure.'

So was that the very end of the Swallows and the Amazons, the Callums and the Death and Glories? Not quite. Part of a thirteenth Ransome novel was discovered by Hugh Brogan among papers lent to Abbot Hall to furnish the drawers of Arthur Ransome's desk. Brogan christened it 'Coots in the North'. Its plot is one which all Ransomites will relish. Joe, Bill and Pete, fed up with the August crowds in Horning, stow away in the cabin of a motor cruiser which is being taken to the lake in the north on a lorry. The idea of doing so was unwittingly that of another old friend from the Broads books, Mrs Barrable.

'Hullo, you three,' said Mrs. Barrable. 'More salvage?' She looked up at the cruiser on the lorry.

'Jonnatt's new cruiser,' said Joe.

'She's going away tonight,' said Bill.

'Voyage by road,' said Mrs Barrable. 'Is she going far?'

All three began talking at once. They told her where the cruiser was going, to the lake at the other end of England, up in the north.

'That Dick and Dot'll be seeing her,' said Pete.

'If they know where she comes from it'll be like getting

a message from the Coot Club,' said Mrs Barrable. 'I'll tell them to look out for her next time I write. Pity you can't make the voyage in her. Come along, William.' And Mrs Barrable walked on through the village without looking back, like one who has dropped a stone into a pool but does not wait to see where the ripples go.

Joe was struck suddenly silent.

'Come on,' said Bill. 'Best have our grub and we'll come back and see her start.'

'Dick put his address on that card they send us,' said Pete. 'We could write and tell them to watch for her.'

'*Bonnka*,' said Bill. 'They'll wonder what her name mean.'

'They know enough Norfolk for that,' said Pete.

'They don't,' said Bill. 'Why when they come here they don't know what a rond be, and that Dick he out with his book and write it down when I tell him the other name for a buttle.'

Joe walked beside them, saying nothing at all.

Joe reveals unexpected powers of leadership and organization, half tricking the other two into turning a brief visit to the cruiser into a serious stowaway, complete with Joe's white rat. When they get close to Bowness (sorry, Rio), they get off the lorry, thinking it has stopped for good, only to find it driving off again. They run down the long road to the lake in pursuit, stopping short for a moment at the sight of the lake,

the crowded bay, the long wooded island outside it, the landing stages for rowing boats, the steamer pier, the moored yachts and motor launches. Far up the lake were two white sails waiting for a breath of wind. Beyond them the great hills that they had seen from far away towered into the evening sky.

'Talk about Wroxham Broad,' gasped Pete.

'That beat Breydon,' said Bill.

They discover that the lorry has already left for the south. All
the security they have left is the motor cruiser, now moored
at Bowness, and Dick and Dorothea's address: Dixon's
Farm. There is a break in the text here, but it is clear from
a sketch of Ransome's that the cruiser's owner proves
friendly – it shows him feeding Ratty milk out of a saucer. In
the last chapter which survives, he takes the boys out across
the lake to look for the Callums. They pass an old blue
houseboat, which is flying an enormous elephant flag, and
the *Bonnka*'s owner says he had a look at it the day before.
' "Rum outfit altogether. They had an accordion going and a
pack of brats dancing on the deck and you'd hardly believe it,

FROM RANSOME'S SKETCHBOOK

but there was a big green parrot screaming at them, perched on the rail round the after deck." ' He lends the Coots his rowing dinghy to get to Dixon's Farm. As they row, they watch three small sailing boats running up the lake. One of them capsizes, but oddly enough the other two sail away instead of helping her. 'Salvage!' shouts Joe, and they row to the rescue. So does another rowing boat, 'pulled by a large stout man, with a bald head on which the sun glinted'. As they close in on the wreck, a head in a bathing-hat surfaces.

Bill made a grab but missed, Joe dropped his oar and grabbed.

There was a shout and violent splashing.

'Got her,' said Joe. 'She's a strong one.'

Slippery with water, the victim twisted under his hands. He lost grip for a moment, but got her by the hair. 'Do I bat her one?' he said.

'Never hold her else. She's gone . . . '

The drowning sailor had twisted over and dived like a seal. Kicking feet showed above the water. Pete got hold of one in both hands.

'Look out! You'll drown her!' There was a shout from one of the other sailing boats, and then, 'Dick! Dick! It's the Coots.'

'Ow!' Pete saw stars. Something enormous hit him on the nose. The next moment a head showed above water a yard or two from the boat.

'Shiver my timbers!' said an angry voice. 'What are you playing at? Tearing my hair out by the roots. Hullo! Did I get your nose? Good.'

The curtain drops tantalizingly at that point, on the exciting prospect of Nancy and the Death and Glories measuring up to each other. Two sorts of pirate, both expert sailors in their own fashion, but with a lot to learn about each other: the romantic versus the practical. Perhaps some day someone will try to finish it. For the moment it seemed right, I decided, as I closed the lid of Captain Flint's Trunk, that

Nancy Blackett should have the last word. Here is a final message written by her, and left in the trunk. I felt on reading it as if I had been tipped the Black Spot myself.

Acknowledgments

My first debts are to Ransome's executors, John Bell and Sir Rupert Hart-Davis, who gave me so much of their time and hospitality, and to Hugh Brogan, whose *The Life of Arthur Ransome* was my starting point and constant touchstone, and who took considerable trouble to answer my questions at a time when he might legitimately have felt he had earned a rest from his labours. The Altounyan family, Taqui, Susie, Titty, Roger and Brigit, were endlessly co-operative in dredging their memories of childhood, and I would like to thank Brigit (now Mrs John Sanders) especially for her enchantingly atmospheric photographs of the Ransome haunts which her family knows so well, and which she took infinite trouble to get right for me.

It was also Brigit who rounded up for me the Altounyan family photographs that appear in the book. Pauline Marshall kindly sent me the photograph of herself and her sister Georgina looking every inch the Amazons she hoped they were, and Josephine Russell let me have her three pictures of the Northern River Pirates on the Norfolk Broads. Richard Pilbow gave me permission to use a still of screen Titty from his *Swallows and Amazons* film, and the Brotherton Library allowed me to plunder 18 photographs from Arthur Ransome's own collection and 13 of the drawings from the celebrated trunk. I am also glad to be able to include two of Clifford Webb's drawings from the first edition (now rare) of *Swallows and Amazons*, as well as drawings by Helena Carter

212

and K.F. Brust from the American and German editions. Unfortunately Dick Kelsall lost the original of Ransome's signalling code through posting it to Cambridge instead of my home in Oxford (his letter was returned to him by the GPO minus its precious enclosure) but luckily a photocopy of it was in existence. Above all I must thank the Ransome executors for their generosity in allowing me to include 20 of Ransome's drawings from his books, as well as 11 others that have never appeared in print before, and to quote at length from his published and unpublished writings. The map of Wetherlam and the endpapers are my own and a few of the photographs were taken with my daughter Tilly's camera.

I am grateful to Taqui Altounyan for letting me quote from her book *In Aleppo Once*, and hope that Myles North will forgive me for giving the game away without so much as a by your leave, all my attempts to trace him having failed. People who knew Arthur Ransome and spoke to me of their reminiscences include Mrs W.J. Backhouse, Jim Clay and his son Jamie, Mr and Mrs Cowcill, Dick and Desmond Kelsall, Sam King, Mrs Cecily Ledgard, Vicky Reynolds (now Mrs McNair), Pauline Rawdon-Smith, Richard Scott and Josephine Russell. I am also greatly indebted to the owners of Ransome's boats who showed me over them and furnished me with photographs and anecdotes: Chris Barlow, Diana Beach, William and Eunice Bentley, and Mrs June Jones.

In the Lake District I was given much help and hospitality by Mrs Sheila Caldwell, Mr and Mrs David Caldwell, Mr and Mrs John Barnes, and Bruce Hanson of Brantwood. I owe a special debt to Mr and Mrs A.H. Connell for the loan of their house in the Winster valley: it was the best workroom I have ever had. On the Broads I have to thank Robin Richardson of Potter Heigham, George Smith of Wroxham, Richard Wood of the Norwich Castle Museum, and most of all Jane Jones, an indefatigable bo'sun for all the frostbite. In Essex I was indebted to the kindness of Peter and Francesca Halliday, Fred and Angie Friedlein and Harry Hawkes. Jo Birley, staunch ally under canvas there, stayed on while I was writing up our adventures at home and made sure that family life survived. The book could not have been written without her.

Sir Michael Clapham introduced me to the Cruising Association's excellent library, a collection in which Ransome himself loved to browse. David Hounslow gave me access to the material in his Ransome centenary exhibition in Blackwell's Children's Bookshop in Oxford. Richard Pilbow and Sophy Neville let me into the filming secrets of *Swallows and Amazons* and the recent television version of *Coot Club* and *The Big Six*, 'Swallows and Amazons for Ever'.

I made extensive use of the unique facilities of the London Library, just as Ransome did, and wandered among its lacy ironwork stacks to find the very copies of obscure maritime voyages which he must once have handled. The staff of the Bodleian Library, Oxford, were extremely co-operative, and I would like to make special mention of Shona Braybrooke and Vera Ryhajlo. Dr Edwardes of Reading University let me browse through the Ransome material in his care. Mary Birkett, director of the Abbot Hall Museum, Kendal, let me work in their 'Ransome corner'. Most indispensable of all has been the enthusiasm of Mrs Ann Farr, custodian of the Ransome archive in the Brotherton Collection at Leeds University (and of Captain Flint's trunk itself). Jonathan Cape, Ransome's own publishers, have been exceptionally supportive throughout the writing of the book, and the specialized knowledge of my editor Tony Colwell has made my work far easier than it would otherwise have been. Linda MacFadyen and Liz Cowen also have my particular thanks.

Two rabid Ransomites, John Hamwee and Saski Huggins, read the book as I wrote it and were invaluable sounding boards and advisers. My husband, Tom Griffith, though not himself a Ransome-reading child, patiently read the stories to our children while I paced the lakeland hills in search of Swallowdale, and brought them to the north the better equipped to be storybook children for a week or two. Finally, of course, without the companionship, enthusiasm, and co-operation of our four daughters Tilly, Daisy, Ellen and Susanna, the quest would have been an empty undertaking.

Bibliography

To write this book I did three sorts of reading. Firstly I read what I could find out about Arthur Ransome, his family and friends, in published and unpublished form. Secondly, I read as many as possible of the books that he himself had read as background to his books. Thirdly I read what he wrote – not only the twelve children's novels, but most of the other thirty or so other published works by him. A full list of those can be found in Hugh Brogan, *The Life of Arthur Ransome*. Here I mention only the most relevant to the writing of the Swallows and Amazons series. So this bibliography is divided into three parts: background reading, Ransome's background reading, and Ransome's own writings. Finally, I include a booklist which Ransome once wrote himself for children who loved his books. Entitled 'Books about Lakes and Pirates', and with his own annotations, it reveals the major influences on his writing for children.

Background Reading

Altounyan, Taqui, *In Aleppo Once*, John Murray, 1969.
Boulton, Helen, *Josephine Crewe*, Longman, 1895.
Brassey, Lady Annie, *A Voyage in the 'Sunbeam', Our Home for Eleven Months on the Ocean*, Longman, 1878.
Brogan, Hugh, *The Life of Arthur Ransome*, Jonathan Cape, 1984.

Brogan, Hugh, 'Ransome's Kingdom', *The Countryman*, Winter 1983/4.

Coles, Kaines Adlard, *Close-hauled: Cruising in the Baltic*, Seeley, Service & Co, 1926.

Collingwood, William Gershon, *The Lake Counties: with Special Articles on Birds, Butterflies, and Moths, Flora, Geology, Fox-hunting, Mountaineering, Yachting, Angling, Shooting and Cycling*, Dent, 1902.

Collingwood, William Gershon, *Thorstein of the Mere, a Tale of Viking Life*, Edward Arnold, 1895.

Davies, George Christopher, *The Handbook to the Rivers and Broads of Norfolk and Suffolk*, Frederick Warne, 1882.

Emerson, Peter Henry, *Life and Landscape of the Norfolk Broads*, Bell & Son, 1888.

Emerson, Peter Henry, *On English Lagoons, being an Account of the Voyage of Two Amateur Wherrymen on the Norfolk and Suffolk Rivers and Broads. With an Appendix, the Log of the Wherry* Maid of the Mist, 1890-1, David Nutt, 1893.

Fox, Uffa, *Thoughts on Yachts and Yachting*, Peter Davies, 1938.

Holland, Eric, *Coniston Copper Mines: A Field Guide*, Milnthorpe, 1981.

Masefield, John, 'Sea-Songs', *Temple Bar*, new series, vols 1 and 2, 1906.

Nixon, W.M., 'Memorable Racundra', *Yachting World*, April 1982.

Ransome, Arthur, *The Autobiography of Arthur Ransome*, ed. and with prologue and epilogue by Rupert Hart-Davis, Jonathan Cape, 1976.

Ransome, Arthur, unpublished writings, diaries, letters and notebooks, Brotherton Library, University of Leeds.

Shaw, W.T., *Mining in the Lake Counties*, Dalesman Books, 1972.

Shelley, Hugh, *Arthur Ransome*, Bodley Head monograph, Bodley Head, 1960.

Smith, Lillian Helena, *The Unreluctant Years: a Critical Approach to Children's Literature*, Penguin, 1976.

Snow, C.P., *Death under Sail*, London, 1932.

Stevens, E. Stefana, *'And What Happened', Being an Account of*

Some Romantic Meals, Mills & Boon, 1916. Written by a literary agent who knew Arthur Ransome as a young man, and modelled her central character on him.

Suffling, E.R., *How to Organise a Cruise on the Broads*, 3rd edn, Jarrold, 1889.

Wainwright, Alfred, *The Outlying Fells of Lakeland*, *Westmorland Gazette*, 1974.

Wainwright, Alfred, *A Pictorial Guide to the Lakeland Fells*, Book Four, *The Southern Fells*, *Westmorland Gazette*, 1960.

Ransome's Background Reading

Arthur Ransome was an exceptionally well-read man. He had a very large library, most of which, sadly for English admirers, is now in California at Fullerton University. His favourite books, however, were given by his wife Evgenia to the Abbot Hall Museum. The list below is of those most immediately relevant to his Swallows and Amazons stories.

Baring-Gould, Sabine, *Mehalah, a Story of the Salt Marshes*, London, 1880. An Essex Romance with something of the cannibal atmosphere of *Secret Water*.

Bullen, Frank T. *The Cruise of the 'Cachalot' Round the World after Sperm Whales*, Beccles, 1898.

Canton, William, *The Invisible Playmate*, Isbister, 1894.

Coward, T.A., *The Birds of the British Isles*, Frederick Warne, 1919-26.

Davies, George Christopher, *The Swan and her Crew: the Adventures of Three Young Naturalists on the Broads and Rivers of Norfolk*, Frederick Warne, 1876.

Davies, George Christopher, *Wildcat Tower: or the Adventures of Four Boys in Pursuit of Sport and Natural History in the North Countrie*, Frederick Warne, 1878.

Eddison, Eric Rucker, *The Worm Ouroboros: A Romance*, Jonathan Cape, 1922. Written by a childhood playmate of Arthur Ransome.

Folkard, Henry Coleman, *The Sailing Boat*, 5th edn, Stanford, 1901.

Giles, Herbert A., *Strange Tales from a Chinese Studio*, London, 1908.

Dixon Kemp, *The Manual of Yacht and Boat Sailing*, 10th edn, Horace Cox, 1904.

Knight, E.F., *The Cruise of the Alerte*. With an introduction by Arthur Ransome, 1890, Rupert Hart-Davis, 1952.

Knight, E.F., *The Cruise of the Falcon: A Voyage to South America on a Thirty-ton Yacht*, Sampson Low, 1884.

Knight, E.F., *The Falcon on the Baltic*. With an introduction by Arthur Ransome, 1889, Rupert Hart-Davis, 1951.

Knight, E.F., *Sailing*, Bell, 1889.

Lynane, C.C., *The Log of the Blue Dragon*, Bullen, 1910.

MacGregor, John, *The Voyage Alone in the Yawl Rob Roy*, with an introduction by Arthur Ransome, Rupert Hart-Davis, 1954.

MacKenzie, Osgood Hanbury, *A Hundred Years in the Highlands*, Edward Arnold, 1921.

Macmullen, R.T., *Down Channel*. With an introduction by Arthur Ransome, Allen & Unwin, 1931.

Masefield, John, *On the Spanish Main*, Methuen, 1906.

Masefield, John, *Salt-water Ballads*, Grant Richards, 1902.

Nansen, Fridtjof, *Farthest North, the Norwegian Polar Expedition, 1893-6*, George Newnes, 1898.

Sabatini, Rafael, *The Sea Hawk*, London, 1915.

Scarborough, William Harrison (ed.), *A Collection of Chinese Proverbs*, Shanghai, 1926.

Slocum, Joshua, *Sailing Alone Around the World*, with an introduction by Arthur Ransome, Rupert Hart-Davis, 1948.

Tambs, Erling, *The Cruise of the Teddy*, with an introduction by Arthur Ransome, George Newnes, 1932.

Wodehouse, P.G., *The Luck of the Bodkins*, Herbert Jenkins, 1935.

Yao Kani, Thomas, *Anansi Stories*, vols 1 and 2, Nelson, 1950.

Books by Arthur Ransome

The twelve children's novels are fully listed with dates and synopses, on pp. 22–6. They were all published by Jonathan Cape.

A History of Story-Telling: Studies in the Development of Narrative, T.C. and E.C. Jack, 1909.

Edgar Allan Poe, a Critical Study, Martin Secker, 1910.

Portraits and Speculation, Macmillan, 1913. A book of literary critical theory.

The Elixir of Life, Methuen, 1915. Well-constructed and pacy historical novel.

Old Peter's Russian Tales, Jack, 1916; reissued by Jonathan Cape, 1984.

The Soldier and Death, J.G. Wilson, 1920.

Racundra's First Cruise, Allen & Unwin, 1923; reissued by Century Books, 1984.

The Chinese Puzzle, Allen & Unwin, 1927.

Rod and Line, Jonathan Cape, 1929.

Introduction to *The Far-Distant Oxus*, by Katharine Hull and Pamela Whitlock, Jonathan Cape, 1937. Ransome shepherded through the publication of this book by two schoolgirl admirers of his books.

Mainly about Fishing, A. & C. Black, 1959.

The Autobiography of Arthur Ransome, ed. and with a prologue and epilogue by Rupert Hart-Davis, Jonathan Cape, 1976.

The War of the Birds and the Beasts, with an introduction by Hugh Brogan, Jonathan Cape, 1984.

Coots in the North and Other Stories, with an introduction by Hugh Brogan, Jonathan Cape, October 1988. (The manuscript of the incomplete story 'Coots in the North' is in the keeping of the Abbot Hall Museum at Kendal.)

Books about Lakes and Pirates

Finally, here is the list which Ransome himself compiled for children who had enjoyed his books and were eager for more ideas about exciting reading, with his comments.

Robinson Crusoe, by Daniel Defoe. This is a very important book for those who want to know what to do on a desert island. It is also good about shipwrecks and voyages.

Thorstein of the Mere, by W.G. Collingwood. This is the story of a Viking boy who discovered Coniston Lake. It was one of my favourite books as a boy. It was a favourite book of the fathers and mothers of the Swallows and Amazons and is now a favourite book of the Swallows and Amazons themselves.

Treasure Island, by Robert Louis Stevenson. This is another of the books that have helped in lots of ways.

The Coral Island, by R.M. Ballantyne.

Midshipman Easy, by Captain Marryat (and others of his books).

Tom Cringle's Log, by Michael Scott.

The works of John Masefield.

The works of Joseph Conrad.

Hakluyt's Voyages.

Sailing Alone Around the World, by Captain Joshua Slocum. Boys who do not like this book ought to be drowned at once.

Small Boat Sailing, by E.F. Knight, who also wrote the Cruises of the *Falcon* and the *Alerte*. Has everything in it that anybody could want to know about sailing small boats.

Bevis, by Richard Jefferies.

Typee, by Herman Melville.

AND

(though much of it may be like a great wind blowing overhead) the greatest of all books ever written:

Moby Dick, by Herman Melville.

Index

221